T0208968

INTO HIS PRESENCE

Tabernacle & The Priesthood

BOBBY HOLMES

WESTBOW
PRESS®
A DIVISION OF THOMAS NELSON
& ZONDERVAN

WestBow Press books may be ordered through booksellers or by contacting:

WestBow Press
A Division of Thomas Nelson & Zondervan
1663 Liberty Drive
Bloomington, IN 47403
www.westbowpress.com
844-714-3454

Scripture taken from the King James Version of the Bible.

ISBN: 978-1-6642-3544-1 (sc)
ISBN: 978-1-6642-3543-4 (hc)
ISBN: 978-1-6642-3545-8 (e)

Library of Congress Control Number: 2021910553

Print information available on the last page.

WestBow Press rev. date: 7/16/2021

Contents

Preface

By Angie Wymer

Bobby and Leta have been precious friends for many years. We attended a Revival together in the 90's and God rekindled a passion in Bobby's heart to learn more about the Old Testament Tabernacle during that trip. I don't believe he knew at that time the in-depth teaching he was going to receive from the Holy Ghost of God.

Our prayer is that you read through this book with an open heart and allow the anointing of the Holy Spirit to reveal Truth to you as you travel back in time to the Old Testament. There is much in the pages of this book that God wants to share with you that are relevant today.

If you are a born-again believer in Jesus Christ, you are now of a Royal Priesthood. Just as the Old Testament priests had responsibilities, the New Testament born again believer has responsibilities today. God has instilled in each of us the ability through the imparting of the Holy Ghost to share the Gospel, the Good News, that Jesus Christ is the Savior of the world and no man can come to the Father but by Him. Jesus died that none would be lost.

You are about to embark on a journey through the Old Testament Tabernacle that will change you forever. Through this book you will learn of the love God has for YOU and how He longs to have relationship with YOU. He has taken care of everything you will ever have need of.

Enter into God's presence with worship and intercessory prayer. As you do, you will be filled with an overflowing abundance of gratitude and love for God and the world that it will be hard for you to leave His presence.

In God's presence you will find anything you have need of and Bobby is going to show you the way as God has revealed it to him, <u>Into His Presence</u>.

Foreword

In 1990, my wife, Leta, and I were attending church at Daisy's Chapel, an Independent Bible Church. The Pastor was Leta's uncle, Frank Nick, Uncle Frank.

Brother Butch Hoffman was the adult Sunday School teacher. The church loved the Pastor and Brother Butch deeply.

Brother Butch began teaching on the tabernacle one Sunday morning. He mentioned the bells and pomegranates, the gold, blue, purple and scarlet red linen. When I heard these words, it grabbed my attention. God sparked an interest in my heart from that moment on.

It's been 28 years now and the interest of the Tabernacle burns within me more now than ever before. God is so good, when He starts something in you, He has a plan. He continues to lead you in that Divine Plan!

In the past few years, I've been working on building the Tabernacle furniture. I have completed the Ark of the Covenant and the Table of Shewbread. The Golden Altar will be completed within the next month and I have hired someone to build the Lampstand by using a 3D Printer Machine. I am also underway, with having the Priestly garment, the Ephod and the Breastplate of Judgment made.

My heart's desire is to build the entire Tabernacle "life-size" someday and I believe God will bless me to do it, for the purpose of teaching. I want people to be able to walk through the Tabernacle, touch it, and visualize where the Glory and Presence of God dwelt and to realize He still dwells in such a place today, and that place is you and I. We are the Tabernacle of God. I Corinthians 3:16, know ye not that ye are the temple of God and that the Spirit of God dwelleth in you.

I'm dedicating this book to the Lord and the Church, God's children, in loving memory of Butch Hoffman and his wife, Sister Patsy,

Brother Butch and Sister Patsy mean so much to me. They are a huge part of my life and I am appreciative of how God used them when He birthed the vision of the Tabernacle in my heart. I love them both!

The Tabernacle and The Priesthood

Who You are In Christ

The Tabernacle is a beautiful teaching showing us how to come into the very presence of God! You will see Jesus all the way through it. You will also find yourself and the body of Christ, the Church, throughout the Tabernacle, even into the Holy of Holies. God's Word is truth and rich in knowledge. We need to cultivate the scriptures. Study them through the Hebrew and Greek original language and begin to know God and become one with Him as He would have us to.

John 17:21-22 That they all may be one; as thou Father, art in me, and I in thee, that they also may be one in us: that the world may believe that thou hast sent me. And the Glory which thou gavest Me I have given them; that they may be one, even as we are one:

We have been clothed in the glory of God that we might be one with Him, and that the world can see Jesus through the lives that we live.

The Law of God and
The Tabernacle

Exodus 20:1, This is when God spoke the Ten Commandments to the people.

Exodus 24:12-18, God spoke to Moses and instructed him to come up Mount Sinai. God was going to give Moses the Ten Commandments that was written by the hand of God. Exodus 31:18

Moses went up Mount Sinai and was there 6 days and on the 7ʰ day God gat (brought – 5927) him up into the Mount; and Moses was in the Mount for 40 days and 40 nights.

There's nothing mentioned about the Ten Commandments within these Scriptures. As you begin Chapter 25 it starts with God telling Moses of all the materials that He wants the Israelites to bring in order to make a Sanctuary for His presence to dwell in.

For the next 6 chapters, God is showing Moses all about the Tabernacle and at the end of their communing in Exodus 31:18, God gives Moses the Ten Commandments that were written with the finger of God.

God spent six entire chapters, 33 days showing Moses the Tabernacle but only one verse on giving Moses the Law. This is not saying that God's Law is of any less importance; after all Jesus said; if you love me you will keep my commandments. The commandments of God are God's Word and are still in full affect today. What God would have us see here is, the Tabernacle teaches us praise and worship. How to come into the very presence of God, and if we would spend the majority of our time in praise and worship, then we wouldn't spend as much time in the do's and don'ts of God's law. Draw close to God and He will draw close to you, love Him, choose Him with every decision you make.

Take notice that God gave Moses Ten Commandments and he wrote them down for Moses, that Moses could teach them unto the people. Exodus 24:12. If Moses needed Ten Commandments written down that he might remember them, then how was he going to remember 6 entire chapters over the course of 33 days, when he was shown the Tabernacle.

Have you ever heard the term a picture is worth a thousand words? Brothers and sisters, Moses saw the Tabernacle that is in heaven.

Exodus 24:18 says he was gat up into the mount. Whether God gave him a vision or took him into heaven itself I don't know, but I do know that Moses saw the Tabernacle.

Exodus 25:9 Moses was instructed to make the Sanctuary according to all that God showed him.

Exodus 25:40 Moses was instructed to make the Table of Shewbread and the Candlestick after the pattern that was showed to him in the mount.

Exodus 26:30 Moses as instructed to rear up the Tabernacle according to the fashion that was showed to him in the mount.

Hebrews 8:2 says that Jesus is the minister of the Sanctuary and of the true Tabernacle, which the Lord pitched and not man.

Hebrews 8:5 Moses was instructed to make the Tabernacle according to the pattern showed him in the mount. "Moses saw the true Tabernacle".

You'll notice that there's two accounts in Exodus of the instructions for building the Tabernacle. The first account is found in Exodus 25-30 when God showed Moses the Tabernacle while in Mount Sinai. This is when Moses received the instructions for building the Tabernacle. The second account is Exodus 35-40 when they built the Tabernacle. The first six chapters (25 – 30) has the quote "Thou shalt make" at the beginning of each piece of furniture being made. The second six chapters (35 – 40) begin with "And they made" so these six chapters were documented as it was built or thereafter.

Who Built The Tabernacle

Moses didn't build the Tabernacle, he was the overseer of it, the Supervisor.

In Exodus 31:2 and 6, God called by name the two men that He chose to build the Tabernacle. Bezaleel and Aholiab are the two men that God put together, as well as all that were wise hearted did God put wisdom that they may make all that God had commanded them.

The Hebrew meaning of the name Bezaleel is "In the Shadow of God".

The Hebrew meaning of the name Aholiab is "Tent of his Father".

Since God joined the two men together and named them by name while Moses was up in Mount Sinai, then I figure we can join the meaning of their names together. I believe God is showing us, this is how we are to build our Tabernacles. Our body is God's dwelling place. "We must be in the Shadow of God in order to be our Father's tent".

Imagine a boy, age 5, walking through the park with his father. The father is holding his hand but the little boy wants to be free.

The father gives his son one rule to follow. He must stay in his father's shadow. Can't you see that little fellow looking at his father's shadow and trying to walk in it. Every now and then looking back at his father to see which way he is going. He would have more fun doing this and he would forget about wandering off.

Brothers and sisters there we are. We must stay in the Shadow of God, in order to be our Father's Tabernacle.

How The Tabernacle Was Built

Exodus 31:3-5 They were filled with the Spirit of God, in wisdom, understanding, knowledge and all manner of workmanship to be able to do a cunning work; a work of craftsmanship. To work in gold, silver, brass, cutting of stones and to carve timber. God wanted a glorious work to be done, the Tabernacle and all of its furniture was to match the one Moses saw while up in Mount Sinai, which is the very same Tabernacle that is in Heaven now. The one that the Lord pitched and not man, Hebrews 8:2, "The True Tabernacle".

In order to do such a glorious work of craftsmanship they were filled with the Spirit of God in wisdom, understanding, knowledge and the craftsmanship of God.

Then how much more do we also need to be filled with the Holy Spirit of God, that we too can build such a tabernacle, a dwelling place for God's presence. We often try to walk this walk in our own strength, all to eventually realize that we must depend upon Jesus and the Holy Ghost of God to see us through, show us the way and enable us to build this tabernacle after the pattern that He gave us. When Moses finished the Tabernacle, Exodus 40:34, says the Glory of the Lord filled the Tabernacle.

Dick Reuben a Jewish preacher quotes "When the pattern is right, the glory will fall". We are to build this tabernacle according to the Word of God, through and by the Holy Ghost of God, not in our own efforts.

When I was about 8 to 10 years of age I stayed with my sister, Donna Holmes, in a farm house just outside of Wytheville, VA. The little one room country church we went to was at the base of Walker's Mountain. The pastor there was Sister Della Umbargar. She was so close to God. She depended on God for everything. In one way she didn't have a whole lot, but in another way she had it all.

She knew Jesus in a special way. I remember that I was afraid to go to the altar and she asked me why one day. I said, "I'm afraid I can't live it, live the life".

She pointed that little bony finger at me and said, "You can't live it and I can't live it. It's what's on the inside that will enable you to live it".

I always thought she meant it's what's in your heart and to a point she did but what she meant was, it's the Holy Ghost that will enable you and I to live such a life that will be pleasing to God.

Brothers and sisters don't try to live such a life in your own strength or your own power. Rely on God and build this tabernacle according to the pattern in His Word.

Well, we are ready to get started into the depths of God's Word. We will go from the Old Testament to the New Testament continuously, cultivating the Word of God, digging into the Scriptures beneath the surface of God's Word, using nothing but the Hebrew and Greek original language. I am using a Strong's Concordance and Old Webster's Dictionary. When we do a word study, I will write the number used in the Hebrew or Greek Concordance.

This way you can take the time you need to study this out thoroughly. It's so important to know why you believe what you do and to know where the Scripture is to back it up.

Jesus overcame the enemy in the wilderness by quoting God's Word. He knew the Word. Jesus is the Word. Jesus said the words that I speak are not my own but that which I have received of my Father. Jesus did the will of His Father and He knew His will because He knew His Word.

Jesus lived His life as being one with His Father and He desires and has instructed us to do so as well. To live as one with Jesus, The Father and the Holy Ghost.

In St John 17:21,22 it says that Jesus put His glory, the very same glory that God the Father put upon His Son. Jesus put that same glory upon us, that we would be one with Him and the Father in order that others would believe that God did send His Son, Jesus, to give them life.

You're not your own, God's presence dwells, lives in you and his glory rests upon you. God is doing a glorious work in you and he's making your life attractive, that others may be able to see Him through you.

"Live in Oneness with God". Love God.

The Courtyard Fence
– Exodus 27:9-19

The Courtyard Fence is a beautiful picture of God's love upon the Old Testament church and even us of the New Covenant church being unable to fulfill the whole Law of God. Being bound by our own sin, standing under the judgment of God. Yet, being delivered by Jesus; the head of the church and committing Himself to us with a love that covers all sin and short comings as well as clothes us in His Righteousness.

There is much more to see here than to just observe a fence. Let's dig deeper together and cultivate the Scriptures, getting the divine revelation that God has inspired in His Word. The intent for us to know Him in a more intimate way. Each step we take, we will be coming closer and closer to the very presence of God, eventually into the Holy of Holies. Let's see God's love for us beneath the surface of the Scriptures.

The Courtyard Fence is 100 cubits long on the north side, 100 cubits long on the south side, 50 cubits long on the west end and 50 cubits on the east end. The circumference of the Courtyard Fence in total is 300 cubits. Exodus 27:18, says the height of the fence is 5 cubits, 7 feet 6 inches tall. Circumference 300 x height 5 = 1500 cubits.

God gave Moses the two tablets of stone, the Ten Commandments, written with the very finger of God. Exodus 31:18, according to the Thompson Chain Reference Bible this took place in 1491 BC.

The Courtyard Fence represents the age of the Law, which was given approximately 1500 BC. In order to see the Body of Christ, the Church, and the love of God in the Courtyard Fence, we need to look deeper into the Scriptures and understand the in depth meaning behind them with the original Hebrew definition.

All of the wood that the Tabernacle and its furniture is built with, represents humanity; mankind.

In Mark 8:24, Jesus put spittle upon a man's eyes and asked him what does he see. The blind man said I see men as trees walking. Jesus touched the man again and he received his sight.

In Isaiah 61:3, says that we might be called Trees of Righteousness, the planting of the Lord, that He might be glorified.

The post of the Courtyard Fence was made of shittim wood, overlaid with brass or copper. Brass or Copper represents judgment, so now you can see the Old Testament church standing there under the judgment of God being unable to fulfill the whole Law of God. If you break the Law in one part, then you've broken the whole Law.

The sockets (bases) of the Post were made of brass or copper, which again represents judgment. Each post was tied down with ropes of goat's hair, and now you can see the people of God, bound by their own sin because they're unable to fulfill the whole Law of God.

God gave these instructions to Moses while he was up in Mount Sinai. Moses was on Mount Sinai for forty days and 40 nights. It was seven days before God spoke to Moses and then he was Gat up (5927) into the Mount, meaning Moses was shown the Tabernacle for the next thirty- three days. Moses not only received the instructions for building the Tabernacle but he was able to see the one in heaven. Study it and look at the details. Gat up (5927) a departure in a northerly direction, an ascension to a higher place.

I'm sharing this detail because there's no mention of the Silver Chapiters, which are the wooden blocks overlaid with silver in the account of Scriptures where God gave Moses the instructions of building the Tabernacle, although there are.

In the second account of the Tabernacle instructions, Exodus chapters 35-40 is when they built the Tabernacle.

In Exodus 38:17 it talks about the Silver Chapiters (7218).

The chapiters being made of wood represent the humanity of Jesus and the silver speaks of His redemption. Jesus came to seek and to save those who are lost. Ephesians 4:15 says that Jesus is the Head, meaning the Head of the church, the body of Christ.

Ephesians 4:14-16, that we henceforth be no more children tossed to and fro, and carried about with every wind of doctrine, by the sleight of men, and cunning craftiness, whereby they lie in wait to deceive;

Vs 15 but speaking the truth in love, may grow up into Him in all things, which is the Head, even Christ:

Vs 16 from whom the whole body fitly joined together and compacted by that which every joint supplieth, according to the effectual working in the measure of every part, maketh increase of the body unto the edifying of itself in love.

We can see the great plan of salvation that God has brought down to man because of His love for us and he could have stopped with this alone but He didn't.

God expresses His love to us even deeper through the Scriptures of how the Courtyard Fence is constructed and held together.

In Exodus 27:10, it says the hooks of the pillars and their fillets (2838) shall be of silver. The hooks are hook shaped anchors or rings made of pure silver and are anchored into the post and the fillets are a rod that slides through them, which is what the hanging of the fine twined linen is attached to.

Fillets (2838) attached, a fence-rail or rod connecting the post or pillars.

Let's look at the same word filleted in 27:17. This Scripture is describing an overview of the Courtyard Fence, but the definition of the word is completely different.

Filleted (2836) to be attached to, love, have pleasure in, delight in.

It has the sense of joining together, adhering, cleaving. This kind of love is already bound to its object.

I can't help but believe we are no longer just talking about a fence row, but God has much more for us to see. God wants us to realize the depth of His love for us, even when we're not able to do everything just right, or falling short in some area. The love that God has for us goes beyond our abilities or inabilities to please Him. He chose to love us first.

Still even now, God has yet another way of expressing His love as well as His seal.

He clothes us in His Righteousness. That's what the hanging of fine twined linen represents, the Righteousness of God.

Revelation 19:8, and to her was granted that she should be arrayed in fine linen, clean and white: for the fine linen is the Righteousness of Saints.

Romans 3:21-24, But now the Righteousness of God without the Law is manifested, being witnessed by the Law and the Prophets; even the Righteousness of God which is by faith of Jesus Christ unto all and upon all them that believe: for there is no difference: for all have sinned, and come short of the glory of God; being justified freely by His grace through the redemption that is in Christ Jesus.

The Entrance of the Courtyard

Exodus 27:14, 15 and 16 The Courtyard Gate was 20 cubits wide (30 feet) and 15 cubits (22 feet, 6 inches) on each side. The gate and the fence were 5 cubits tall (7 feet, 6 inches). God's people had to encamp a good distance away from the Courtyard Fence and with the fence being so tall, it had to be very disappointing to say the least, to not be able to see what's going on inside the Courtyard Fence. Although they were able to see the Glory of God by watching the pillar of fire by night which no doubt had a shiny glow upon the Silver Chapiters.

I like to compare the Scripture in Titus 2:11 "For the grace of God that bringeth salvation hath appeared to all men".

The Gate of the Courtyard was the only way in.

John 14:6 Jesus said "I am the Way, the Truth, and the Life, no man cometh unto the Father but by Me". The gate was the only way in. The door of truth is the first veil covering separating the courtyard (place of judgment) and the Holy Place.

The Veil represents the life, the life of Jesus, the entrance into the Holy of Holies.

We will see more on this later as well as the color of linen the gate is made from. The Veil and Door of Truth were made the same way with the same colors but we will study this as we study the Veil.

The Brazen Altar

Exodus 27:1-8, The Brazen Altar is all about Jesus and what He did for us. There's a beautiful description within these eight verses of the sacrifice of Jesus. Every detail portrays Christ and the depth of His love for us and the Father. There are many things to bring out and study within these eight verses, so please study the detail with me and see these beautiful treasures that's just beneath the surface of God's Word.

Proverbs 4:7, Wisdom is the principal thing, therefore get wisdom: and with all thy getting get understanding.

Understanding the depth of the Word of God will cause a more intimate relationship with our Heavenly Father, the Lord Jesus Christ and the Holy Spirit of God. To know Him in a more intimate way will cause us to be more like Him and enable us to love others at a deeper level.

The Brazen Altar will also lead us to the Scriptures about the Priesthood. We will follow this path because the Priest were the only ones that were allowed inside the Tabernacle and as we move ahead we will be coming closer and closer to His presence. We need to recognize who we are in Christ, and whom God has made us to be. I Peter 2:9, But ye are a chosen generation, a royal priesthood, an holy nation, a peculiar people; that ye should shew forth the praises of Him who hath called you out of darkness into His marvelous light.

We're not just studying the Priesthood of old, we're taking on the Priesthood that we have been brought into. God has so clothed us in the Priestly Garments for a purpose: to enter into His presence not only for our own sakes but that we may intercede on the behalf of others, that are not allowed into the Holy of Holies. We must recognize who we are and who we are in Christ.

To know the power and authority that's been vested in us and given to us that we might be one with Him.

John 17:21-22 "That they all may be one; as thou, Father art in Me, and I in Thee, that they also may be one in us; that the world may believe that thou hast sent Me. And the glory which thou gavest Me, I have given them; that they may be one, even as we are one".

The very same glory that was upon Jesus while He was here with us, has now been placed upon us, that we might be one with Him, in order for others to see Christ in us. We have become sons and daughters. II Corinthians 6:18

God would have us come into His presence with confidence and boldness, knowing who we are in Christ. Understanding the depth of sacrifice that was made for you and I will establish our hearts and minds in Christ with an assurance and His seal of promise, which will cause us to have his blessed assurance. This will no doubt, spill over into your persistent love for others. To reach into their lives at a deeper level of concern and love that you could never have possibly done on your own. This is still in effect today. Not in the natural as it was in the Old Testament but in the spiritual.

Interceding on behalf of others that know nothing about being in the presence of an Almighty God! You've been equipped with such power, love, and compassion, deeper than you've ever known on your own. You've taken on the mind of Christ, the will of God.

God would have us come boldly into His presence, not with arrogance but with confidence and assurance because we know Him. What He's done for us and who we are in Christ because of His great work of salvation.

Hebrews 10:19-20, Having therefore, brethren, boldness to enter into the Holiest by the blood of Jesus, by a new and living way, which He hath consecrated for us, through the veil, that is to say His flesh.

We have access by faith through the blood of the Lord Jesus Christ into the Holy of Holies. We have been given privileges that no other generation has been given. We can come directly into the very presence of God! We must put on this calling, take on this position that God has brought us into. Let's move forward, understanding every detail that God is sharing with Moses about the Brazen Altar, and about all of the Tabernacle, for every detail is there for a purpose. God would have us know Him at a deeper level not only for us ourselves but for others as well. You have been called and placed into this priesthood for a reason.

There are priestly duties that must be fulfilled and all of us, "God's children", have been equipped with this power, love and compassion from on high. We all know who we are, now let's recognize who we are in Christ and glorify Him with our living in the newness of life that He has called us into.

As we study the Priesthood and how we've been brought into it, we will also study the Garments of the Priesthood and how we are clothed in them. The garments of salvation, righteousness, and we've been endued with power from on high; meaning clothed upon with the Holy Ghost!

We've been made in the image of God and after His likeness, so we are being brought into an intimate relationship with Him not only for ourselves but for the purpose of others to be saved and to know Him as well.

Please study the details of Scripture with me going forward and see Jesus!

Exodus 27:1-8, The Brazen Altar was made of shittim wood which represents the humanity of Christ, overlaid with brass (copper) which represents judgment.

II Corinthians 5:21, For He hath made Him to be sin for us, who knew no sin, that we might be made the righteousness of God in Him.

The size of the altar was 5 cubits long and 5 cubits broad by 3 cubits tall. That's 7 feet 6 inches by 7 feet 6 inches foursquare X 4 feet 6 inches tall. If you were to take one of the boards of the Tabernacle structure, which is 15 feet tall by 27 inches wide, and cut it in half, stand it upon its edge with it being 7 feet 6 inches long and 27 inches tall. The two cut boards laying horizontally and stacked on top of one another is 7 feet 6 inches long by 4 feet 6 inches tall, the exact size of the Brazen Altar.

Jesus took on humanity, became just like us with the exception, He didn't have a sin nature.

Hebrews 2:14-18, For as much then as the children are partakers of flesh and blood, He also Himself likewise took part of the same, that through death He might destroy Him that had the power of death, that is, the devil; 15) and deliver them who through fear of death were all their lifetime subject to bondage, 16) For verily He took not on Him the nature of angels, but He took on Him the seed of Abraham, 17) Wherefore in all things it behooved (necessary) Him to be made like unto His brethren, that He might be a merciful and faithful High Priest in things pertaining to God, to make reconciliation for the sins of the people. 18) For in that He Himself hath suffered being tempted, He is able to succour them that are tempted.

Jesus was made like unto us that He could experience and feel the pain and sorrow that we feel, the hurt and loneliness, the emptiness and the abuse from others, as well as the joy, gladness and comfort from our Heavenly Father.

Jesus wanted to feel our hurts and sorrow that He could be there with you in your troubled time and give you the mercy and comfort as well as the power that's needed to bring you through it.

Jesus is our great High Priest. He intercedes to God the Father on our behalf.

Hebrews 2:9, Jesus was made a little lower than the angels for the suffering of death, crowned with glory and honor, that He by the grace of God should taste death for every man.

We no longer have to fear death, Jesus conquered death, hell and the grave!

John 10:17-18, "Therefore doth my Father love me, because I lay down my life, that I might take it again.

18) No man taketh it from me, but I lay it down of myself. I have power to lay it down and I have power to take it again. This commandment I have received of my Father".

The Tabernacle boards that are 15 feet tall by 27 inches wide made of shittim wood, represent the church, the body of Christ. One of these boards being cut in half makes the exact size of the Brazen Altar on one side, which represents Jesus laying down his life for us.

John 10:10, Jesus said that He came that we might have life and have it more abundantly (4053)

Abundantly (4053) beyond; beyond the normal, supernatural …

Jesus gave His all, His life, that we could be set free from bondage. The penalty has been paid. He paid a debt that we could not pay and He gave us power to become the sons and daughters of God.

Psalm 24:7-10, Lift up your heads, O ye gates; and be ye lifted up, ye everlasting doors; and the King of Glory shall come in.

8) Who is this King of Glory? The Lord strong and mighty, the Lord mighty in battle.

9) Lift up your heads, O ye gates; even lift them up, ye everlasting doors; and the King of glory shall come in.

10) Who is this King of Glory? The Lord of Host, He is the King of Glory!

We have joy unspeakable and full of glory, have a merry heart and recognize what Christ has done for you. Live in the power of His resurrection, walk in the newness of life that He has provided for you. Live in the abundance of the Holy Spirit of God, which lives in you. Recognize the goodness of God and whom He has made you to be.

Leviticus 17:11, For the life of the flesh is in the blood: and I have given it to you upon the altar to make an atonement for your souls.

We've not received the blood of bulls and goats but we've received the blood of Jesus, which not only frees us from the bondage of sin, but it also breaks the power thereof and enables us to live a life that's pleasing to the Father.

Now we will go deeper still into the Brazen Altar seeing the depths of God's love through the sacrifice of Jesus. See the extent of His love through the details that is given.

Exodus 27:4-5, And thou shalt make for it a grate (4345) of network (4640) of brass; and upon the net shalt thou make four brazen rings in the four corners thereof.

Grate (4345): A Covering

Network (4640): Operative, exerting power or force

Verse 5: and thou shalt put it under the compass (3749) of the altar beneath, that the net may be even to the midst of the altar.

Compass (3749): A rim, top margin (ledge)

The Grate of Network of Brass made of solid copper, representing judgment was placed just beneath the compass ledge that wrapped the outside of the altar and down to the ground on each side of the altar as a protective covering.

The animals of sacrifice were tied to the horns of the altar and they would kick against the grate and it would prick or sting their hooves.

Jesus said, "Saul, Saul, why persecutest thou Me, it is hard to kick against the pricks". (To fight against God's will)

To see the importance of the compass (ledge) of the altar we need to study the sacrifice in Leviticus 1:4-9. This will also lead us into the Priesthood.

Let's go Scripture by Scripture to get a good understanding of what's being done and what this means for us today. We could start in verses 6-9 but verses 4 and 5 are necessary for us to know going forward.

Leviticus 1:4 and "he" shall put His hand upon the head of the burnt offering, and it shall be accepted (7521) to make atonement for him, pay off, pardon, delight in. The word "he" is the person that brought the sacrifice, not the priest.

Leviticus 1:5 and "he" shall kill the bullock before the Lord: and the priest, Aaron's sons, shall bring the blood and sprinkle (2236) the blood round about upon the altar that is by the door of the tabernacle of the congregation.

Notice "he" the person who brought the sacrifice, shall kill the sacrifice. The person that brought the sacrifice took ownership of taking the life of the animal. This made it personal. Then the priest took the blood and ministered. The blood was sprinkled round about the altar. Sprinkle (2236) To pour out.

To pour out life's blood, represented there's no greater sacrifice than this, that a man would lay down his life for his friends and Jesus said we are his friends. It represents an unbreakable bond between God and man because there's no greater sacrifice.

Leviticus 17:11, For the life of the flesh is in the blood: and I have given it to you upon the altar to make an atonement for your souls; for it is the blood that maketh an atonement for the soul.

Leviticus 1:6 and he shall flay the burnt offering, and cut it into his pieces.

Leviticus 1:7, and the sons of Aaron, the priest, shall put fire upon the altar, and lay the wood in order upon the fire;

Leviticus 1:8, and the priest, Aaron's sons shall lay the parts, the head, and the fat, in order upon the wood that is on the fire which is upon the altar:

Leviticus 1:9, but his inwards and his legs shall he wash in water: and the priest shall burn all on the altar, to be a burnt sacrifice, an offering made by fire, of a sweet savor unto the Lord.

There's an incredible amount of detail that God has inspired to be written in the Scriptures describing the sacrifice and how it was to be done. Notice the wood had to be placed in order.

According to Exodus 27:8, the altar was hollow on the inside, not having a grate as some pictures show the Brazen Altar. The grate was on the outside as a protective covering as we've already studied.

I struggled with the meaning of the order of the wood, just couldn't find anything on this that would tie in or could give me the meaning of this in Scripture. Then one day in study, God made it so simple, He said "the order of the wood was placed in order to hold the sacrifice".

The sacrifice was cut into pieces in order to cleanse it, wash it and get the fat which provided a sweet aroma, and the sacrifice had to be placed back in its order and offered as a sacrifice to God.

What's done in the Old Testament is a shadow of what's to come in the New Testament. Jesus died upon the cross and the wood was placed in order to hold the sacrifice.

That was a beautiful amount of detail shown in the Old Testament Scriptures and Jesus fulfilled every one of them in the New Testament.

Now we need to also see the importance of the compass/ledge of the altar. Knowing now that the sacrifice had to be placed in order and the size of the Brazen Altar was 7 feet 6 inches by 7 feet 6 inches and 4 feet 6 inches tall, that was a nice size altar. For the sacrifices to be placed in order they would have to get upon the ledge and walk around the altar to reach from each side to accomplish this. To see this in Scripture look at Leviticus 9:22.

Leviticus 9:22, and Aaron lifted up his hand toward the people, and blessed them, and came down from offering the sin offering, and the burnt offering and the peace offerings.

Notice Aaron was upon the ledge of the altar and before coming down he lifted his hand toward the people and blessed them. Aaron was the high priest, and we know Jesus is our Great High Priest today, so let's see how Jesus fulfilled even these Scriptures in the New Testament. Jesus was not only the perfect, sinless Sacrifice, He was also the High Priest.

Luke 24:50, and He led them out as far as to Bethany, and He lifted up his hands, and blessed them. Jesus blessed them even as it had been taking place for years, fulfilling the Scriptures in every way. He blessed them with the Priestly Blessing in Numbers chapter 6.

Numbers 6:24-27, The Lord bless thee, and keep thee: the Lord make His face shine upon thee, and be gracious unto thee: The Lord lift up His countenance upon thee, and give thee peace.

There's one more Scripture to share in Revelation 1:15. His feet was like unto fine brass, as if they burned in a furnace … Showing that He was that Perfect Sacrifice for us.

Brothers and sisters, Jesus fulfilled every part for us. He loved us beyond our comprehension. He left nothing undone. The Scriptures are written for our learning and everyone of them are meant to be for instruction, correction, and to build us up in the faith that God has established in us.

We must be able to know the foundation that our faith stands upon. We need to know the foundation of the Gospel from the Old Testament to the New Testament.

We've all been guilty of saying, yea I know it's in there somewhere, I just don't know where it is myself, but I've heard it all my life. We've been taught this and that all of our lives.

Brothers and sisters, Jesus defeated the enemy with the Word. The very Word which He received from His Father. It's important for us to know the Word. Going forward we are going into an extensive study of the Priesthood. How the Priesthood was established with Aaron and his sons. How it was passed down to Jesus and how we have been brought into the Priesthood today and for what purpose. We will also study the Garments of the Priesthood at this time. We need to study the Priesthood at this time because only the Priest were the ones that were allowed inside the Tabernacle.

Therefore, we need to know who we are in Christ, whom He's made us to be and for what purpose before we can enter into His presence and truly appreciate the Glory of God that we've been given and that we will walk in as we walk through the Holy Place and then on into the Holy of Holies.

It's a beautiful, wonderful blessing for us to be saved and to be able to come into the very presence of God, but all of this isn't just for us, it's for others.

The Priesthood

I Peter 2:9, But ye are a chosen generation, a royal priesthood, an holy nation, a peculiar people; that ye should shew forth the praises of Him who hath called you out of darkness into his marvelous light.

We've been brought into the Priesthood through a blood birth, being born again, now of the Tribe of Judah; a direct descendant of Jesus!

Numbers 18:7, Therefore thou and thy sons with thee shall help your priest office for everything of the altar, and within the veil; and ye shall serve: I have given your priest office unto you as a service gift: and the stranger that cometh nigh shall be put to death.

The Priesthood is a gift of service that's been given to us to minister to others. We've been bought with a price, ye are not your own. God has endued us with power from on high and has equipped us with tools of righteousness.

Our members of our bodies are now members of His Body and have become instruments of righteousness, (Romans 6:13).

We have been given the access, the ability, the permission to come into the very presence of God.

Hebrews 10:19-20, Have therefore, brethren, boldness to enter into the Holiest by the Blood of Jesus, by a new and living way, which He hath consecrated for us, through the veil, that is to say, His flesh; and having an High Priest over the House of God; let us draw near with a true heart in full assurance of faith, having our hearts sprinkled (4472 pour, creating an unbreakable bond) from an evil conscience, and our bodies washed with pure water.

The priest would sprinkle, pour the blood round about upon the altar, the Brazen Altar. Leviticus 1:5, Creating an unbreakable bond between God to man, because there's no greater sacrifice than one's life, all has been given.

Hebrews 10:22, says having our hearts sprinkled from an evil conscience …

The precious Blood of Jesus not only cancels the debt of our sin and forgives us but it also purges, cleanses, purifies our conscience from dead works so that we can serve our Living God.

Hebrews 9:14, How much more shall the Blood of Christ, who through the Eternal Spirit offered Himself without spot to God, purge your conscience from dead works to serve the Living God.

It's important for us to know who we are in Christ, who He's made us to be. We are His sons and daughters, we've been forgiven, redeemed, born again, that we can walk in new life, walk in His resurrection; even as he came out of the tomb, we can walk in the newness of life. We fight a battle within, we need to recognize it for what it is, it's a spiritual battle. Our new born again spirit lives inside of these fleshly bodies and it creates a battle because we have a sin nature.

We're born with a sin nature, but when we received our Lord Jesus Christ as our personal Savior, we received a new nature; old things are passed away and behold all things have been made new. We still have a sin nature and we will until we leave these fleshly bodies, but that sin nature must die daily and we must learn to walk in our new nature of Christ that we have received through Christ Jesus.

You and I have received our Lord Jesus Christ through Divine Revelation, Divine Intervention. God revealed Himself to you and me. God set all things aside to reveal Himself to you and me. All of heaven was focused right there upon you at the time of your salvation and you left the old man sitting in his or her place and you entered into a Spiritual setting, a place in God, where God caused you to understand that He is God and that Jesus gave His life for you that you might have life and have it more abundantly. Man did not reveal God to you, God Himself reached into the depths of your soul to cause you to understand enough about salvation to know that you needed Him and to cause you to be able to believe in the Virgin Birth, Crucifixion, and Resurrection of our Lord Jesus Christ. God planted that within you, stamped it, sealed you with the Holy Spirit of Promise. Now have become a son or daughter of God!

Your journey of growth and knowing Him begins, you grow, gain more knowledge, your love for God deepens and you start to realize you've been called to minister to others. You've been called into the Priesthood, which is very much alive today. We've been given access into the very presence of God through the blood of Jesus, Hebrews 10:19-20. This access into God's presence is not just for us alone but it's also for others.

You've been given this access by your faith in the Lord Jesus Christ; through the shed blood of our Lord Jesus Christ and God has revealed Himself to you. Not everyone has this, they've not had this experience.

They've not received this Divine Revelation that caused you and me to understand about the Great Salvation. You and I need to carry them before God! Yes, to bear their load, cry aloud in prayer that they might come to understand who God is and that they might be led to the way of the cross as you and I were. You can't reveal God to them, only God can do that, but you can carry them before Almighty God and present their name to Him and pray for God to draw them and cause them to understand.

We must first study how the Priesthood was passed down from the descendants of Aaron of the tribe of Levi to Jesus which is of the tribe of Judah and the importance of that change. That change was for us, He took on a Priesthood after the order of Melchizedek, "The power of an Endless Life".

He ever liveth to make intercession for us, and therefore we are saved to the uttermost, Hebrews 7:25.

Once we see the change in the Priesthood and the Scriptures that support it, we will see how we've been brought into the Priesthood and even clothed in the Priestly Garments. We will study the importance of the Priestly Garments and which ones we are wearing. That's correct, you're already wearing some of them and have been commissioned to put the others on as well.

The Priesthood was established with Aaron and his sons as an Everlasting Priesthood, Numbers 25:13.

The Priesthood was passed down to the descendants of Aaron from generation to generation by reason of death, Hebrews 7:23.

Numbers 18:1, Aaron, his sons and his father's house with him was to bear (5375) the iniquity of the Sanctuary and of the Priesthood. Bear (5375) to lift, carry or pardon

The purpose of the Priesthood was to bear the sin of the people, to carry the weight of their guilt and shame. To make a sacrifice and present the shed blood before God for an atonement, which was a shadow of the shed blood of Christ, which was to come.

I Chronicles 24, gives an account of the Priest, the descendants of Aaron.

Now let's see where the Priesthood is at the New Testament. Luke 1:5, Zacharias was a Priest of the Course of Abiah or Abijah: see I Chronicles 24:10, which was a direct descendant of Aaron. Elizabeth was of the Daughters of Aaron and through the prayers of Zacharias and the Ordained Plan of God, they were blessed to be with child. The angel, Gabriel, told Zacharias to call his name John.

The angel, Gabriel, that stands in the presence of God, told Zacharias that John would be great in the sight of God and would be filled with the Holy Ghost even from his mother's womb. John would turn many of the children of Israel to the Lord, showing them the way, and to make ready a people prepared for the Lord.

Jesus said in Matthew 11:9-11, that John was more than a prophet … This is he whom it is written, "Behold I send my messenger before thy face, which shall prepare thy way before thee. Verily I say unto you, among them that are born of women there has not risen one greater than John the Baptist: not withstanding he that is least in the kingdom of Heaven is greater than he".

John was brought directly into the Priesthood as a descendant of Aaron and as chosen by God. To carry one's load, to turn the hearts of the people toward God. To prepare the people to come to know the Lord Jesus Christ. Truly fulfilling the duties of the Priesthood.

Exodus 29:1-9, To be dedicated into the Priesthood, they had to be hallowed, (consecrated, made holy, set apart) to minister in the priest office. A sacrifice had to be made and Moses had to wash Aaron and his sons at the Door of the Tabernacle and then put the Garments of the Priesthood upon them. They were already wearing the linen breeches, the undergarment but the other garments Moses had to put upon them.

The white linen coat, (Robe of Righteousness), the Robe of the Ephod (Holy Ghost), the Ephod, the Breastplate, gird with the girdle of the Ephod and place the Mitre on their head and place the Holy Crown upon the Mitre.

John the Baptist having received the Priesthood by a blood birth, a direct descendant of the sons of Aaron and by the ordained plan of God, was chosen to prepare the way for the Lord to come. Turning, preparing, the people's hearts to hear and receive of our Savior, the Lord Jesus Christ.

John said, "He must increase and I must decrease".

Matthew 3:13-17, John, being humbled for he knew what must take place, he knew he was to baptize Jesus, one who was so mightier and to be esteemed more than He, but because Scripture was to be fulfilled, John obeyed and baptized Jesus. Notice the words spoken by Jesus: "Suffer it to be so now: for thus it becometh us to fulfill all <u>Righteousness</u>".

Matthew 27:37, Jesus' accusation, which was written upon the Cross was: This is Jesus The <u>King</u> of the Jews.

Jesus took on a Priesthood after the order of Melchizedek, which is the power of an endless life. The name Melchizedek in Hebrews 7:2 says the interpretation of the name Melchizedek is <u>King of Righteousness</u>.

When John the Baptist, baptized Jesus it was the passing down of the Priesthood. John, so to speak washed Jesus in water as Moses did Aaron and his sons at the Door of the Tabernacle to consecrate them into the Priesthood. John, baptizing Jesus was to fulfill all Righteousness, to fulfill the will and ordained plan of God.

Hebrews 7:11-17, there was a change made in the Law. The Priesthood was established with the tribe of Levi, the Levitical Priesthood but under this Priesthood nobody could be made perfect. No one could be totally free from sin because the blood of bulls and goats was not worthy enough to take away sins, but only to make an atonement, a covering for them. Under the Old Covenant the sacrifice would not clear the conscience and therefore the person would still carry their guilt and shame.

God made this change in the Priesthood through his ordained plan of salvation that we would not only be forgiven of all sin, but that even our conscience would be cleansed, made pure, that we can serve our Living God, verse 14. That we might receive the promise of eternal inheritance.

Jesus was not only that Perfect Sacrifice but He is also our Great High Priest.

Hebrews 9:24, Jesus entered into the Holy of Holies with His own blood to present before God, not the Holy of Holies made with men's hands, but into the very Throne of God in heaven, the True Holy of Holies.

Brothers and sisters, receive this truth, this freedom from the power of sin and shame. You have been set free through the Ordained Salvation Plan of Almighty God, that even your conscience can be made pure from the guilt of sin and shame.

Rejoice in whom God has made you to be, live in His resurrection power, walk in His truths. You have been vested in the Kingdom of God, through the impartation of the Spirit of Almighty God. Ephesians 1:14, you have received the earnest (portion) of your inheritance until the redemption of the purchased possession unto the praise of His glory ... Rejoice, again I say Rejoice ...

Recognize the glory of God that has been revealed in you. This is the very same glory that was upon Jesus while here on this earth.

John 17:21-23, That they all may be one, as thou Father, art in Me, and I in Thee, that they also may be one in Us; that the world may believe that thou has sent Me. And the glory which thou gavest Me I have given them; that they may be one, even as We are one: I in them, and Thou in Me, that they may be made perfect in one; and that the world may know that Thou has sent me, and hast loved them, as Thou has loved Me.

Brothers and sisters, we have been made one with God the Father, Jesus the Son through and by the power of the Person of the Holy Spirit of God and the precious blood of the Lord Jesus Christ.

Live and walk and breathe in this glory that you've been given. Realize that this is bigger than you and I. This is God's Ordained Plan that we have been blessed to be brought into and we must realize the purpose of such a privilege that we've been given.

Jesus said He gave His glory, not just glory, but the very same glory that God the Father gave Him, He gave to us ... for the purpose that we would be made one with them, not being equal to, but in agreement with, being made like unto them in our living, in our thinking, in our doing. Old things are passed away, behold all things have become new.

God has equipped us to overcome through His finished work at Calvary.

Jesus said He gave us His glory that we would be made one with them and that the world may know and believe that God has sent Jesus.

Brothers and sisters, we have been brought into this Divine Plan of Salvation that others would be able to see Christ Jesus in us, that they too could be saved.

John 3:16, For God so loved the world, that He gave His only begotten Son, that whosoever believeth in Him should not perish, but have everlasting life.

The Priesthood doesn't end at this point, even as God told Aaron and his sons it would be an everlasting Priesthood and so it is. God has brought us into this everlasting Priesthood, with Jesus being our Great High Priest, Hebrews 4:14.

Brothers and sisters, knowing we've been given the glory of God and being made one with God as well as being brought into a Royal Priesthood, let's see the Scriptures that we can have knowledge of in order that we can stand upon God's Word to know who we are in Christ.

The Church Being Consecrated into the Priesthood

John 13:1-20, Jesus knew that His hour was come, He was to depart from this world and go to His Father. Jesus knew the Father had given all things into His hands; authority, power, the kingdom of heaven and the very glory of God was upon Him.

Jesus knew He came from God and it was time to return to God. Jesus rose from supper and proceeded to fulfill the Father's Word.

Jesus took on the Priesthood, past down and ordained through the baptism of John, even as Moses washed Aaron and his sons, John washed Jesus through baptism in the Jordan to fulfill all righteousness.

Jesus' hour was come, it was time to ordain the disciples into the Priesthood. Jesus didn't pass down the Priesthood, for He became the Great High Priest after the order of Melchizedek; the power of an endless life; a Priest forevermore to make intercession for us before God the Father, that He can save us to the uttermost.

Jesus didn't pass down the Priesthood, but He brought us into a Royal Priesthood with Him and ordained us through the washing of our feet. Humility at its finest, yes and servanthood with no greater demonstration. What better way could Jesus show those whom He loved to give this same love to those whom they will minister to. Even as Numbers 18:1, says Aaron and his sons were to bear the iniquity of the Sanctuary and of the Priesthood.

Jesus brought the disciples into this Royal Priesthood, they were to take on these duties of the Kingdom of God. Jesus told Peter, "you know not what I do unto you now, but you shall know hereafter". The disciples grew, took on this ministry, it became their life, who they were in Christ Jesus.

Now that we have been washed and ordained into the Priesthood we will now see the Scriptures where God has clothed us with the Priestly Garments. Even us, those of us beyond the day of the Cross have been washed by the water of the Word, to sanctify, to make holy and consecrate for Himself a glorious church, Ephesians 5:26-27.

John 19:34, But one of the soldiers with a spear pierced His side, and forthwith came there out blood and water.

Hebrews 10:22, Let us draw near with a true heart in full assurance of faith, having our hearts sprinkled from an evil conscience and our bodies washed with pure water.

The Garments of
the Priesthood

Exodus 28:2, and thou shalt make Holy Garments for Aaron, thy brother, for Glory (3519) and for Beauty (8597).

Verse 4: These are the Garments which they shall make; a Breastplate, and an Ephod, and a Robe, and an Broidered Coat, a Mitre and a Girdle, and they shall make Holy Garments for Aaron, thy brother, and his sons, that he may minister unto Me in the Priest's office.

These are the Garments that God had Moses to clothe them in. Notice they didn't put these Priestly Garments upon themselves but Moses was instructed by God to wash them and clothe them. With the exception of one Garment, which was the Linen Breeches, an under garment. See Exodus 28:42-43

The Linen Breeches were to be upon them already; meaning they were to put these on themselves. Verse 43 says, that they wear these, so they bear not iniquity and die.

The Linen Breeches were the only Garment that they had to step into and pull upon themselves. All the other Garments were put upon them from above, over the head or upon the shoulders.

The Linen Breeches represent Salvation, which each and every individual will have to step into themselves, no one can do this for you.

Then God clothes you in His Righteousness, which is the White Linen, Embroidered Coat.

Isaiah 61:10, I will greatly rejoice in the Lord, my soul shall be joyful in my God, for He hath clothed me with the garments of Salvation, he hath covered me with the Robe of Righteousness, as a bridegroom decketh himself with ornaments, and as a bride adorneth herself with her jewels.

Once we stepped into Salvation, put those Linen Breeches on, God washed us clean, whiter than snow and clothes us in the Robe of Righteousness. Preparing us for the Marriage Supper of the Lamb …

Every priest wore these Garments as well as the Girdle which held the Robe snug at the waist, and the Mitre or Bonnet.

These Garments were worn that they could minister unto the Lord in the Priest Office. They were hallowed (set apart, consecrated) unto the Lord through the sacrifice, the washing/cleansing at the Door of the Tabernacle and clothed with these Garments.

To minister unto the Lord is to worship and praise Him but it's also to serve others. The Priests were the only ones allowed in to the Tabernacle, near the Holy things of God. How special they must have felt, how close to Almighty God knowing that His presence abode just to the other side of the Veil. They must have been cautious, quiet, reverent and careful as well as respectful while so near to God.

Know this brothers and sisters of God, they were there in the place of others, for others could not come in. Others did not have permission, they did not have access, they were not equipped or prepared to come into the presence of Almighty God, but the priest were and therefore they were to bear the Iniquity of the Sanctuary and of the Priesthood, Numbers 18:1.

They were to bring the hearts, lives, the hurts and the sins of the children of Israel before the presence of Almighty God and get the sin under the blood for atonement, lift up the broken and the hurting as they offered incense upon the Golden Altar that sits closest to the Veil, which we know represents Jesus' body.

See, brothers and sisters what you and I have been brought into, surety of no less importance than any other time in history. We have been so clothed in this Salvation and ... Oh God adorned in His Robe of Righteousness, prepared and dressed to meet the Bridegroom; our Father which is in Heaven ..., but realizing with this special gift of ministry also comes the responsibility of caring for others. We have been given access into the very presence of God, not just into the Courtyard, and into the Holy Place, but into the Holy of Holies. We not only have access into the Holy of Holies, but Hebrews 10:19-20 says that we can have boldness when we enter into the Holy of Holies because of the blood of Jesus.

Brothers and sisters, we're not entering into the Holy of Holies made with hands of the Old Testament, no we're of a Royal Priesthood. We're entering into the true Holy of Holies, into the very presence of God in Heaven. We've been made to sit together with Him in heavenly places in Christ Jesus our Lord, Ephesians 2:6.

Recognize the glory of God that is upon you, the Holy Spirit that lives within you and the Garments that God has clothed you in. You only put on Salvation (Linen Breeches), God clothed you with the rest and He did it for a purpose, that you and I would join with Him, become one with Him and minister unto the Lord by serving others.

You and I both have family members and friends that don't know God ... take a moment and think of what that means, don't become calloused and noncaring but weep instead that they might know God. You can't do it for them but you can bring their name before Almighty God and plead for them. You see, they don't see what you see, they don't know what you know or who you know, they're just living life as you and I once did. How empty, how dreadful, they don't have that Blessed Hope that you have to come to know, that gives you joy unspeakable and full of glory. The peace you have even though everything else goes bad.

Follow the example of our Lord and Savior, Jesus Christ.

Hebrews 2:17-18, Wherefore in all things it behooved (necessary) Him to be made like unto His brethren, that He might be a merciful and faithful High

Priest in things pertaining to God, to make reconciliation for the sins of the people. For in that He Himself suffered being tempted, He is able to succour them that are temped.

You've entered into a Royal Priesthood and are able to come into the very presence of God, without hesitation, know that you are His and He is yours, being made one with Him.

He loves others just as much as He loves you and me. We used to be others. Take on this Priesthood that God has brought you into and care for others as you minister unto Him.

Garments of the High Priest

Your first thought as you begin to read this section of the Priestly Garments is, this will have nothing to do with me, but quite the opposite is true. Everything mentioned in the previous passage about the Priestly Garments of caring and reaching others will be times ten in this passage and to our surprise during New Testament times the Church, the Body of Christ has been clothed in these Garments as well.

Scripture must interpret Scripture. We need to see how this comes about in Scripture so we have a sure foundation to stand upon.

This is so important for us to know how God has equipped us and for what purpose. How far can we go, how close can we be, who are we in Christ. God said in Exodus 19:6, "you shall be unto Me a Kingdom of Priests". Which also ties in with 2 Peter 2:5 and 9, Revelation 1:6.

Exodus 29:5, And thou shalt take the Garments, and put upon Aaron the Coat, and the Robe of the Ephod, and the Ephod, and the Breastplate, and gird him with the Curious Girdle of the Ephod.

We must study these Garments individually, their meaning, their function, their purpose to understand the importance of their purpose today in our lives. These have to do with how you will bring your loved ones into God's presence. God has equipped us with His love and so we must put on Christ that others will come to know Him.

As we study the Robe of the Ephod, we will touch on other Scriptures that tie in with Jesus taking on the Priesthood and proving that he who had the title as High Priest was not the High Priest of God.

We will also see how God has so allowed us to be clothed with such a Garment that only the High Priest wore in the Old Testament, but now with the New Covenant in place, we have been permitted to wear this Garment spiritually as well as the other two Garments, the Ephod and the Breastplate. There's much detail to share, much Scripture to go through and study, but as we do, we will have the foundation of God's Word to stand upon to know "Who we are in Christ and whom He's made us to be".

The Robe of the Ephod

Exodus 28:31-35

And thou shalt make the Robe of the Ephod all of blue. And there shall be a hole in the top of it, in the midst thereof; it shall have a binding of woven work round about the hole of it, as it were the hole of a habergeon that it be not rent.

The Robe of the Ephod had a hole in the top of it for the head. It was put on from above. Around the neck area there was a work of woven material to re-enforce it from being torn. There was a penalty for tearing the Priestly Garment and the penalty was death, Leviticus 10:6.

Matthew 26:62-65, The people didn't understand the quote that Jesus made, that He could destroy the temple, build it again in three days. The High Priest at that time was Caiaphas and he said unto Jesus, "answer thou nothing?".

But Jesus held his peace. Jesus fulfilling Scripture by staying silent.

Isaiah 53:7, He was oppressed, and he was afflicted, yet he opened not his mouth: He is brought as a Lamb to the slaughter, and as a sheep before her shearers is dumb, so he openeth not His mouth.

Matthew 26:63, The High Priest answered and said unto Him, "I adjure Thee by the Living God, that thou tell us whether thou be the Christ, the Son of God". Jesus began to speak here because again to fulfill Scripture and that He would not break the Law.

Leviticus 5:1, If a soul sin and hear the voice of swearing, and is a witness, whether he hath seen or known of it; if he does not utter it, then he shall bear his iniquity.

Matthew 26:64, Jesus saith unto him, "Thou has said: never the less I say unto you, hereafter shall ye see the Son of Man sitting on the right hand of Power, and coming in the clouds of Heaven".

Then the high priest rent his clothes saying …

I will stop there because he shouldn't have been able to say anything. The penalty for tearing these Garments was death and he didn't die because he wasn't God's ordained High Priest, Jesus was. Jesus had already taken on this Priesthood from the baptism of John and was fulfilling His Father's will.

Moving forward we will see the Bells and Pomegranates on the bottom of the Robe and study their function and meaning in the New Testament. Jesus wore this Garment spiritually and we will see that we've been blessed to wear this Garment as well. Keep in mind there was a hole in the top of it and it was put on from above, over the head.

Exodus 28:34-35, and beneath upon the hem of it thou shalt make pomegranates of blue, and of purple and of scarlet, round about the hem thereof; and bells of gold between them round about: a golden bell and a pomegranate, upon the hem of the Robe round about.

A pomegranate is a fruit and it represents the Fruit of the Holy Spirit of God: love, joy, peace, longsuffering, gentleness, goodness, faith, meekness, temperance.

Between each pomegranate was a golden bell which would ring as it touched the pomegranate as the priest would move throughout the Holy Place.

Exodus 28:35, and it shall be upon Aaron to minister: and his sound shall be heard when he goeth in unto the Holy Place before the Lord, and when he cometh out, that he die not.

I Corinthians Chapter 13 is called the Love Chapter:

Though I speak with the tongue of men and of angels and have not charity, I am become as sounding brass or a tinkling cymbal. And though I have the gift of prophecy and understand all mysteries, and all knowledge, and though I have all faith, so that I could remove mountains, and have not charity, I am nothing.

The Golden Bells represent the Gifts of the Holy Spirit of God and the Pomegranates the Fruit of the Holy Spirit of God. Without the Pomegranates between the Bells it would have been as Paul described; as sounding brass or a tinkling cymbal. Everything we do in Christ is to be done through the love that God has established in us.

I Corinthians chapters 12 and 14 are both Bell Chapters; speaking of the Gifts of the Spirit. Chapter 13 is the Love Chapter.

This is not a coincidence that these three chapters are in this order. This is the inspired Word of God!

Exodus 28:35, says Aaron was to wear this Robe to minister, and sound shall be heard when he goeth unto the Holy Place before the Lord, and when he cometh out, that he die not.

Brothers and sisters there's to be noise in the church. The Gifts of the Spirit through the love of God are to be in full operation in the church, that we die not!

We know the disciples received the Gifts of the Spirit after they received the Baptism of the Holy Ghost. Jesus told the disciples this was to come, let's see this in Luke 24:49. "And behold, I send the Promise of My Father upon you: but tarry ye in the city of Jerusalem, until ye be endued (1746) clothed upon, invest with clothing, with power from on high."

The Promise of the Father is the Baptism of the Holy Ghost; the Robe of the Ephod, all of blue, with Golden Bells and Pomegranates round about the hem of it representing the Baptism of the Holy Spirit.

Turn with me through the Scriptures and see this Glory we've been given. We must recognize the goodness of God and what He's brought us into. We need to wear these Garments with honor and yet with humility. We are truly the children of God!

Acts 1:3-8, Jesus showed Himself alive for forty days after his passion (crucified), by many infallible proofs and speaking of the things pertaining to the Kingdom of God. Being assembled with the disciples, He told them not to depart from the City of Jerusalem but to wait for the Promise of the Father.

Verse 5: For John truly baptized with water; but ye shall be baptized with the Holy Ghost not many days hence.

Verse 8: But ye shall receive power after that the Holy Ghost is come upon you: and ye shall be witnesses unto me both in Jerusalem, and in all Judea, and in Samaria, and unto the uttermost parts of the earth.

The disciples knew Pentecost was coming, it was celebrated all their lives. Pentecost was a Feast Day. A Feast Day, ordained by God as being fifty days after the Feast of First Fruits which we know represents the Resurrection of our Lord Jesus Christ. All of this is found in Leviticus Chapter 23, the crucifixion, resurrection, Pentecost, day of atonement, and the return of our Lord Jesus Christ.

The disciples also knew they were to prepare for the Day of Pentecost because according to the Law they brought bread with a new meat offering, which was leaven mixed in with the bread. The leaven did not represent sin at that time of the Old Testament it represented time. It took time to prepare bread with leaven because you had to work it in the bread and then let it sit to allow it to rise.

The Spiritual leaven that they brought was time. Jesus showed Himself alive for forty days and then told them to wait in Jerusalem until they receive the Promise of the Father, the Baptism of the Holy Ghost.

Acts 1:12-15: The 120 went back to Jerusalem, to the upper room and continued with one accord in prayer and supplication, for there were ten days left until Pentecost was fully come.

They received the Baptism of the Holy Ghost and began to speak with other tongues as the Spirit gave them utterance.

The Cloven Tongues of Fire sat upon each of them.

Brothers and sisters, we have been endued with power from on high, that we can minister unto the Lord through and by the love of God bearing the load of many, that they too might be brought to the knowledge of knowing the Lord Jesus Christ.

We truly have been blessed to wear this Robe of the Ephod. There are the Gifts of the Spirit and they're to be demonstrated and in full operation through the love of God today that we may minister to others.

Notice in Exodus 28:35 where this Garment was worn; in the Holy Place, not in the Holy of Holies.

The Holy Place represented the church age. We will see that as we study the Lampstand, the Table of Shewbread and the Golden Altar.

The Robe of the Ephod wasn't worn in the Holy of Holies because in heaven no one will need healing, no one will have cancer, there will be no need for interpretation of tongues or prophecy. We will be with Jesus and we will be made like Him; incorruptible, no more sin, no more sorrow.

Leviticus 16:4, will give us the requirements for the Garments that are to be worn into the Holy of Holies. They are the Linen Breeches, the white embroidered Robe, the Girdle and the Mitre. The other Garments, Robe of the Ephod, the Ephod, and the Breastplate of Judgment are all for the church age.

We see how we've been clothed with the Robe of the Ephod, but what about John the Baptist and Jesus. John the Baptist received the Holy Ghost even from his mother's womb and Jesus received the Holy Ghost at the Baptism of John.

Matthew 11:4, Jesus answered and said unto them, "Go and show John again those things which ye do hear and see; the blind receive their sight, and the lame walk, the lepers are cleansed and deaf hear, the dead are raised up and the poor have the gospel preached unto them".

Yes, Jesus wore this Garment, The Robe of the Ephod, but He wore it in the Spirit as an example unto us, and so we must as well move through the Spirit of God and make sure the sound of the Gifts of the Spirit through the love of God is heard today as we minister unto the Lord in this priest office, To reach those whom Jesus gave His life for. With whatever gift and calling of God that is upon your life, do it all to the glory of God, giving yourself wholly unto Him. Hold nothing back, ye are not your own, you've been bought with a price. You are the Temple of God, that He dwells in.

Brothers and sisters, if we have been permitted to wear such a Garment as this Robe of the Ephod, that only the High Priest was allowed to wear in the Old Testament, then we must realize we've also been permitted to put on the Ephod and the Breastplate of Judgment. Now we will step deeper into the Priesthood and the responsibility of bringing others before God, that they too might know Him.

Brothers and sisters, we have been made in the image of God and after His likeness. We are to be one with Him according to John 17:21-23.

Let's move forward to the Ephod and the Breastplate of Judgment with the 12 stones as well as the Urim and Thummin to see what God has brought us into and for what purpose. Let's recognize who we are in Christ. Whom He's made us to be and for what purpose.

The Ephod

Exodus 28:5-30

There's an incredible amount of detail and description of the Ephod and how it was made.

The Ephod was worn over the Robe of the Ephod and the Breastplate of Judgment was attached to it, over the chest area.

David knew the importance of the Ephod, when Saul came after him. David had Abiathar, the Priest, bring the Ephod to him and David began to pray about the battle he was to face, I Samuel 23:9 and I Samuel 30:7.

Ephod (646) High Priest Shoulder Piece, also an Image

This is the Hebrew definition in the Strong's Concordance. It describes the Ephod as being the Shoulder Piece Garment, but it also says an Image.

Genesis 1:26 and God said, "let us make man in Our Image, after Our likeness ..."

Verse 27, So God created man in His own Image, in the Image of God created He him, male and female created He them.

We were created in the Image of God and after His likeness. John 17:21-23, says the very same glory that God gave to Jesus, Jesus gave to us, that we may be one, even as They are one. The Ephod was the Garment that the Breastplate of Judgment was attached to, which had the 12 precious stones set in place over the heart. Each of the 12 stones represented one of the 12 tribes of the children of Israel.

There were also 2 onyx stones placed on the Shoulders and had 6 of the tribe's names engraved into each stone as well as the 12 stones over the heart which had their names engraved into them. This enabled the High Priest to carry the 12 tribes of the children of Israel in before the Lord, over his heart and on his shoulders, fulfilling their Priestly duties, what God had commissioned them to do in Numbers 18:1, to bear the iniquity of the Sanctuary and of the Priesthood.

The High Priest carried these 12 tribes before God into the Holy Place as he wore the Breastplate of Judgment, for their names were engraved into those precious stones, which were placed by God, to be over the heart and upon the shoulders.

This is symbolic of how we are to carry those of our loved ones, friends, and all those who we know are lost and without God. We are to fulfill Numbers 18:1; bear the load and carry them to Jesus. Having them upon our hearts and yes even our shoulders, that they may come to know the love of God. There is a specific way this is to be done, through prayer of course and we will study much deeper into this as we study the Golden Altar and the incense that was offered up to God. Let's look deeper yet into the Breastplate of Judgment, what God has given us, to be able to present these, who we bring before Him.

The Pastor of my youth was Sister Della Umbargar. To me being just a little fella of about ten years old, I always saw her as being about 70 or 80. I had told her, I didn't come to the altar because I was afraid that I couldn't live it, and she pointed that little bony finger at me and said, "you can't live it and I can't live it, but it's what's on the inside". I had always thought she meant it's what's in your heart and to a point she did, but what she meant is, it's the Holy Ghost. The Holy Ghost will enable you to live such a life. He will lead you and guide you into all truth. He will cause you to be more than a conqueror in Christ Jesus. The Holy Ghost will enable you to be more than you are in yourself. You are not your own, you've been bought with a price, to glorify God, and He will cause you to walk in all of His ways. See Ezekiel 36:27

Truly, we can not live such a life on our own and of ourselves. We aren't meant to. God will enable us and God will receive the glory. Neither can you live it for someone else or carry their load of sin and shame or sorrow on your own. You must rely on God and the Spirit of God that lives in you.

This is why we need to look deeper still into the Breastplate of Judgment, into a Pocket that was made behind the Stones in the Breastplate.

Brothers and sisters, it's all here in the Word of God, we don't have to figure it out. God already has established the way.

Exodus 28:30, and thou shalt put in the Breastplate of Judgment the Urim (224) and the Thummin (8550) and they shall be upon Aaron's heart, when he goeth in before the Lord and Aaron shall bear the judgment of the children of Israel upon his heart before the Lord continually.

Urim (224/217) Lights, an oracular brilliancy of the figures in the High Priest Breastplate.

(217): flame, fire

Thummin (8550) Perfections; the object in the High Priest Breastplate as an emblem of complete truth.

The Urim and Thummin was placed into the Pocket of the Breastplate of Judgment, which was behind the 12 stones that represented the 12 tribes of the children of Israel.

They were to be upon Aaron's heart when he was going in before the Lord, into the Holy Place and Aaron was to bear the Judgment of the children of Israel upon his heart before the Lord continually. The <u>Urim</u> and <u>Thummin</u> represented <u>lights, fire</u> and <u>compete truth</u> and <u>perfection</u>.

As Aaron came before the Lord bearing the Judgment, carry the load of the 12 tribes and their many circumstances before God, no doubt he had to be able to discern and weigh the matters that he brought before God.

He needed much more than his own discernment or his own thoughts about the matters brought before him, he needed to rely upon God.

The Thummin represented the Holy Ghost, which leads us and guides us into all truth.

The Urim represents the Fire of the Holy Ghost. Brothers and sisters, we have also been permitted to have the Urim and the Thummin in these Garments that we are wearing, but they are Spiritual Garments and so the Thummin is the Holy Ghost that we have been baptized in, starting on the day of Pentecost. The fire that fell upon each of them is the Urim, which will cause us to be able to live this life before them who know not God. We will be able to discern the matters that are brought our way because we are not relying upon ourselves, but upon God.

We house the Holy Spirit of God and have been equipped and given the power to become the sons and daughters of God. We've entered into a Royal Priesthood, one not of this world, but of the Kingdom of God. Live in oneness with God, know who you are in Christ and whom He's made you to be. Share what's been shared with you.

Can you imagine the light from the Urim that was placed inside the Pocket of the Breastplate of Judgment along with the Thummin, shining out against those precious stones; Sardius, Topaz, Carbuncle, Emerald, Sapphire, Diamond Ligure, Agate, Amethyst, Beryl, Onyx and Jasper.

I don't know what object was used for the Urim, the Light, but it must have been a sight to see it shining from the back side of these stones, causing the stones to glitter, sparkle and glow. This my brothers and sisters, is how we are to carry others before God. On our shoulders, on our hearts and through and by the Holy Spirit of God. God will supply you with that kind of love for others as you and I grow more and more in love with Him. Love others through God's love. Even as the Hebrew definition of the word Ephod describes the priest's garment and also says an image.

As we minister to others and carry them before God, we then bear the image of God. Interceding upon their behalf. We bear the image of God, for we are the Priest of the Most High God, a Kingdom of Priests and a Royal Priesthood. We are to still offer sacrifices, which are the fruit of our lips giving thanks unto God and the lifting up of our hands as the evening sacrifice. Recognizing who we are in Christ, who He's made us to be. Let's move forward to the Laver, the Door of the Tabernacle and into the Holy Place.

The Laver

Exodus 30:17-21, 38:8

The Laver was placed between the Altar and the Door of the Tabernacle. Aaron and his sons were to wash their hands and their feet at the Laver before they came near the Altar or the Tabernacle, that they die not. There was space between the Altar and the Laver and another space between the Laver and the Tabernacle. As they ministered in their priestly duties their hands and feet would get dirty and needed to be cleansed. I call this area, life. The world in which we live, yet not a part of.

Exodus 38:8 says the Laver was made of looking glasses of the women. Their mirrors were made of polished copper, which the women gave so the Laver could be made. The Laver was filled with water and as they would look into the water they could see their reflection of themselves because the copper of the Laver was polished.

Ephesians 5:26-27, that He might sanctify and cleanse it with the washing of the water by the Word, that He might present it to Himself a Glorious Church, not having spot or wrinkle or any such thing; but that it should be holy and without blemish.

The water represents the Word of God, which provides us a daily cleansing as we're here in this world. Hebrews 10:22, let us draw near with a true heart in full assurance of faith, having our hearts sprinkled from an evil conscience, and our bodies washed with pure water.

The Door of the Tabernacle

Exodus 26:36-37

The Door was a hanging of blue, purple, scarlet and fine twined linen, which separated the Holy Place from the Courtyard. It was made of the same materials as the Veil and the Gate of the Courtyard. We will study these colors of linen when we go over the Veil, which represents Jesus' body. The Door was hung from five pillars made of shittim wood. The wood represents mankind, they were overlaid with gold. The gold represents the glory of God.

There were five sockets of brass or copper made for these posts; the sockets are the brass that the post sit on; the foundation. The brass or copper represents judgment. When we studied the Courtyard Fence, we saw that it represented mankind being unable to fulfill the whole Law of God, being bound by their own sin; standing there under the judgment of God, for the Post and their Sockets were of brass or copper.

The five posts that the Door hung from were overlaid in gold, but their sockets were of copper. I believe this would represent mankind trying to keep/fulfill the whole Law of God (Genesis, Exodus, Leviticus, Numbers and Deuteronomy), yet being unable to; for there was only One who could do that and that is Jesus. These five posts were still within the area of the Courtyard, therefore the Sockets, the foundation that they sat upon were the judgment of God. You must walk through the Door of the Tent and then the very foundation of your faith will be the redemptive work of our Lord Jesus Christ, the finished work at Calvary.

This Door is called the Truth. Jesus said in John 14:6 "I am the Way, the Truth and the Life: no man cometh unto the Father but by Me". The Gate of the Courtyard is the only way into the Courtyard, the Door is the Truth and the Veil that represents Jesus' body is the Life, which He gave for us, that we might have life more abundantly.

The Tabernacle Structure

The Tabernacle building, the boards that make the Tabernacle structure represent the church, the body of Christ. They're made of wood overlaid in gold; the glory of God and their sockets; their bases are made of solid blocks of silver which represents redemption.

The Scriptures will show a beautiful picture of God's love for His church, the body of Christ and us as individuals, as we are, as we have been made to be in Christ. There's an incredible amount of detail that God has had written for our learning about His love for us in the Scriptures. It not only tells of the ones who are standing tall and strong, but the Scriptures also tell of the ones who are weak and the hurting, as well as what the church is to do about it.

Really, could we still be talking about the Old Testament Tabernacle? Yes, brothers and sisters, we are. God has given all of this to us in His Word, His plan of salvation, His great love, wherewith He loved us.

Please study this with me and every detail that God has put in place because of His love for us.

Have you ever seen Grandma pick the meat from a chicken to make a stew? There's nothing left, right? Nothing but the bones ...

That's what we're going to do in these Scriptures. We're going to get every morsel of meat that God has provided for us to have.

The boards were 10 cubits tall and a cubit and a half wide, which is 27 inches wide and 15 feet tall. Being made of wood, they represented mankind. They were overlaid (6823) with gold.

Shittim wood (7838), (7850), (7752)

7838: Scourging thorns

7850: To Pierce

7752: To flog, goad, scourge

The shittim wood reminds us of what Jesus went through for us while He was here in His humanity even as we are, and we too will have to go through some things, how much, we know not. Jesus physically laid his life down and we too must spiritually lay our lives down, that we might have life and have it more abundantly.

Overlay (6823) Expansion in outlook, to peer into the distance.

Romans 4:17 God calls those things which are not, even as though they were.

The Boards were overlaid in gold, the glory of God. God sees us as what we will be as if we already are … that's love.

The foundation of each board was two sockets of solid silver. The boards were 27 inches wide, that's 2 feet, 3 inches wide, so each socket had to be 13 ½ long, so they would be continuous, end to end.

Exodus 26:17-21, says there were two sockets under one board and 2 tenons (3027) in one board. There was one tenon for each socket of silver.

Tenon (3027) a hand, power, strength, assistance

Each one of the boards had two sockets of silver to sit on as a foundation which represented the redemptive work of Christ at Calvary and each socket of silver had a tenon, a pipe of some kind or a piece of wood that come up out of the socket of silver and into the bottom of the board; holding the board secure in its place. Two tenons in every board, the two hands of God; Jesus and the Holy Ghost holding us secure in the redemptive work of Christ.

Once we step through the Door of the Truth the very foundation that our faith rests upon, is the redemptive work of Christ, our Lord and Savior. We are not our own, we have been bought with a price. Each one of the sockets of silver was made of one talent which is 75 pounds each piece, Exodus 38:27.

The boards were placed one against another on the North, South, and West end of the Tabernacle. Twenty boards on the North, twenty boards on the South and eight boards on the West end. The Tabernacle was 15 feet wide and 45 feet long. If you take 6 boards and put them in place across the West end, you'll have 13 feet, 6 inches, leaving a dimension of 18 inches.

The Bible says there were 8 boards across the back, so they had to cut a board down to a 9-inch width for each side, which made it to be 15 feet.

Exodus 26:25, scripture says there's to be 8 boards and 16 sockets of silver. This is just like the North and South sides except for the two corners. They are only 9 inches wide which means the two sockets of silver had to be shaped different from all the others, since they too were made the same as the others, with one talent of silver according to Exodus 38:27.

These two, 9 inch wide, boards being much smaller than all the rest of the boards were placed at the two corners of the building. These smaller boards were placed here, so they would have the support of the full-size boards on each side of them. These two smaller boards also represent mankind. Maybe when we don't feel like we measure up to someone else's standard, or sick, or even hurting, from some type of hardship. God knew that there would be times that we all would face hardships and circumstances, where we needed the support of others, so He places us at the strongest part of the building.

Since this was a corner and the board was only 9 inches wide, the 75 pound, sockets of silver were shaped to fit the corner as well as to meet up against the sockets on the North and South sides. This means the socket of silver would have been extended out beyond all the others, giving it a more secure foundation.

Isn't that awesome, just like God. He thought of it all and put it in His Word, just for us. He could have stopped right there with such a glorious message but he didn't.

Exodus 26:24 "and they shall be coupled together (8382) beneath, and they shall be coupled together above the head of it unto one ring: thus shall it be for them both; they shall be for the two corners".

Coupled together (8382) To be complete, to be doubled, paired, to be twins, duplicate.

These two 9-inch boards were joined together with the other full-sized boards at the bottom and the top by a ring, so they could be secure and be able to stand even as all the others were. Saints, this is how we are to support the hurting, the lowly or maybe it's just someone who's been through some hardships for a while. God has made a place for them in the Tabernacle structure and it's in a corner, so they can be joined to brothers and sisters of like precious faith, so that they might receive comfort, support and love from the family of God. We all will have our times in those corners and we will need the loving support of our brothers and sisters in Christ to help us stand. This is the example that God has given us, His divine plan, His example. When the pattern is right, God's glory will fall.

There's one more thing we need to see that God is showing us with the Tabernacle structure. It is the Five- Fold Ministry of God.

The boards were 27 inches wide, 15 feet tall, sitting on 75-pound solid blocks of silver with 2 tenons (hands) coming up into each one of them, which means that board had to be at least 3 inches thick. Even though it had such a good foundation and the boards were so big and beefy, they would all be out of line with one another towards the top of the building.

Exodus 26:26-29 There were five bars of shittim wood placed on each side and the West end. There were two bars a few feet down from the top, two bars a few feet up from the bottom and one bar across the middle reaching from one end of the Tabernacle to the other. There were three rings in each board and the bars would slide through the rings. There are a total of forty-eight boards, 20 on the North, 20 on the South and 8 on the West end.

There were three rings in each of the forty-eight boards which gives us 144 rings, representing the 144,000 that the book of Revelation speaks about. The bars slid through these rings and held the boards in line together.

This prevented the boards from beginning to bow and stayed in a straight line with all the others. The five bars represent the five-fold ministry of God found in Ephesians 4:11-16, "and He gave some Apostles, and some Prophets, and some Evangelists, and some Pastors, and Teachers: for the perfecting of the Saints, for the work of the ministry, for edifying of the body of Christ: till we all come in the unity of the faith, and of the knowledge of the Son of God, unto a perfect man, unto the measure of the stature of the fulness of Christ: that we henceforth be no more children, tossed to and fro, and carried about with every wind of doctrine, by the sleight of men, and cunning craftiness whereby they lie in wait to deceive; but speaking the Truth in love, may grow up into Him in all things, which is the head even Christ; from whom the whole body fitly joined together and compacted by that which every joint supplieth, according to the effectual working in the measure of every part, maketh increase of the body unto the edifying of itself in love".

Brothers and sisters, we have been called to be there for brothers and sisters of like precious faith, which may need to be restored. To reach out, to build up, to encourage.

It's been such a blessing to me to see all that God has for us in the Scriptures about the Tabernacle. It's all about Jesus and it's a pattern for us to live our lives by, that we might bring forth the praises that are due unto His name, and for us to know His divine plan of how we're to come into His presence. There's yet much more to share. We will move forward now to the Holy Place, the Furniture, the Veil, and the Ark of the Covenant, which is in the Holy of Holies.

Only the priests were allowed into the Holy Place. The priest had to first wash their hands and feet before they entered the Door of the Tent. They had to offer up sacrifices and be dressed in the Priestly Garments that Moses ordained them in. We to, being the Priest of God must do these same things. God is the same yesterday, today, and forevermore. The priestly duties then were a shadow of what was to come.

As we come into God's presence, we must examine ourselves, visit the Cross and stop at the Laver for our spiritual cleansing. This, even as then, is to be done daily, lest we die spiritually. We must recognize who we are in Christ and the Garments that He has clothed us in, for the purpose of worship and to minister to others. Forgetting not that the foundation of your faith rests upon the redemptive work of Christ Jesus, the finished work at Calvary, not upon your own goodness or your own righteousness, for we have none, we have been redeemed. We are His and He is ours. We are made one with Him.

The Lampstand

Exodus 25:31-40

The Candlestick or Lampstand was the only thing in the Holy Place that gave light in order for the priest to be able to see. It was made and all the vessels they used to tend to it with one talent of solid gold, which is 75 pounds.

It had one main stem at the center, called the Candlestick and 6 branches, 3 on each side. In each branch there was a bowl, a knop and a flower. The bowl was shaped as an almond and placed as the calyx of a flower, the knop encircled and joined two branches and the flower blossomed just above them. There were 4 sets of them in the center Candlestick, which would make 12 ornaments. There were 3 sets in each one of the 6 branches, so each branch had 9 ornaments.

Taking the count of ornaments into the center stem which is 12 and add the ornaments in the 3 branches side, which is 27 ornaments in the 3 branches on the left, adds up to be 39 ornaments.

The 3 branches on the right side also had 27 ornaments. This totals up to 66 ornaments in all. There are 66 Books in the Bible, 39 in the Old Testament and 27 in the New Testament.

Psalm 119:105, Thy Word is a Lamp unto my feet and a light unto my path.

The Lampstand represents the Word of God, for it's the Word of God that provides light to us while we're living here in this world.

The ornament (bowl) that was shaped like unto an almond was to represent the quick work of God that His Word will do in a person's life, even as a vile wretched sinner, sits and hears the Word of God preached, his heart moved and is drawn to an altar of repentance and moments later has become a brand, new person, everything from the inside out has been made new, they're free, born again. Old things are passed away and behold all things have become new. This my brothers and sisters, is the quick work of God and to God be the glory. There was no time to make one's self ready, to prepare, to become a better person or to quit the fleshly sinful habits but instead a genuine heavenly transformation has taken place. One has gone from the paths of hell and has been redeemed, changed, made new and made ready for the kingdom of heaven … glory be to God, Oh, my Jesus, I love Him so … Only God can do a work as this. This is divine intervention, heavenly impartation, that can change a person in such a quick moment, even as God will take us home to be with Him. We will be changed in a moment in a twinkling of an eye, forever to be with the Lord.

The almond tree is one of the first to bloom in the Spring. Jeremiah 1:11-12, Jeremiah answered the Lord and said "I see a rod of an almond tree" and God said "thou hast well seen for I will hasten my Word to perform it".

The Lampstand's center stem called the Candlestick had a place below the branches called a Shaft (3409). It was a place for a man's hand to take hold of it and carry the light with him as he ministered within the Holy Place.

Shaft (3409) thigh, haunch, loin, side

Genesis 24:9, Abraham's eldest servant, made an oath with Abraham, that he would bring a wife to Isaac his son from his home country. The oath was done by placing his hand under Abraham's thigh and commit to Abraham's request.

The Shaft of the Lampstand uses this same word. By placing one's hand around the Shaft to carry the Lampstand, the Light of God, it represents us carrying the Word of God and committing to Him in the strongest oath known to man, that we will commit to keeping His Word.

John 20:27-29, Even as Jesus told, whom we call doubting Thomas, Jesus said, "Reach hither thy finger, and behold my hands; and reach hither thy hand and thrust it into my side: and be not faithless but believing." and Thomas answered and, said unto Him, "My Lord and my God". Jesus saith unto him, "Thomas because thou hast seen me, thou hast believed: blessed are they that have not seen, and yet have believed".

Jesus allows Thomas to commit and assure himself by placing his fingers, oh, my Lord, into the nail holes of His hands and to put his hand into his wound, where the spear pierced His side while on the Cross. Jesus didn't call him doubting Thomas, but saw the imperfection and addressed it by allowing him to assure himself and be restored. What love saints, my Jesus, love Him so …

One may think, the nail prints and the wound in His side would have been gone away, after all, Jesus was showing Himself alive after His resurrection.

Revelation 5:6 describes Jesus as a Lamb that had been slain.

Brothers and sisters, I believe the nail prints and the wound in His side will be there for us to behold, when we see Him. Jesus has a glorified body, so there's no pain, but yet has preserved us the opportunity to behold Him and His great love for us. I can't say enough, can't find words to describe this moment in eternity that we will be blessed with, to behold him: Jesus, the Lamb of God!

Hold to the Truth, the Word of God and commit your life unto Him as He has committed His life unto us and our Heavenly Father. Be not faithless, but believing. "Blessed are they who have not seen, but yet they believe".

The Table of Shewbread

Exodus 25:23-30

The Table of Shewbread was placed on the North side (right side) within the Holy Place. It was made of shittim wood and overlaid with gold. It was 36 inches long, 18 inches deep and 27 inches tall. Its purpose was to hold the Shewbread.

Keep in mind as we study each piece of Furniture, the wood represents humanity and the gold the glory of God. The word overlay, speaking of the wood that's overlaid in gold, reminds us of the Scripture in Romans 4:17. God calls those things that are not even as though they are.

There's a crown around the perimeter of the table and there's a Border (4526) of a hand breadth round about and a crown also placed on the Border.

Border (4526) enclosing, <u>a close place</u>

The Border was built a hand width closer to the Center of the Table, roughly 4 inches in width closer to the Center of the Table. Inside of this Border is where the Shewbread is placed, which is at the Center of the Table.

Luke 24:30-31, the two men on the road to Emmaus sat and ate with Jesus, and as Jesus broke the bread and gave them to eat, their eyes were opened and they knew Him.

As they ate of the bread, Jesus was revealed to them. This is the <u>Close Place</u> where Jesus would have us be, that we may know Him.

All of the dishes that were made for the Table were made of pure gold and the Shewbread was to be upon the Table, always. The Table that held the Shewbread represents us, clothed in the glory of God and living at a Close Place with Jesus that we may know Him and everything that we allow in our lives needs to be of the purest, even as the Gold, that the Bread may always be upon us, which is Jesus.

The Golden Altar

Exodus 30:1-6

The Incense Altar was made of shittim wood, overlaid with gold, representing humanity covered with the glory of God. It was 18 inches by 18 inches foursquare and 36 inches tall, with a crown of gold round about. There were horns overlaid with gold on each corner, which pointed out to the north, south, east and west. There were two rings placed upon two corners, opposite each other. This is a place for the staves/poles to slide through for the purpose of carrying the altar as they traveled through the wilderness.

The purpose of the Golden Altar was to burn incense upon it, Exodus 30:1, Aaron was to make an atonement upon the horns of it once a year with the blood of the sin offering.

Exodus 30:6, It was placed just before the Veil, which we know the Veil represents Jesus' body. The Golden Altar was the Closest piece of Furniture to the Veil and its purpose was to burn incense thereon.

Psalm 141:2, David says, "let my prayer be set forth before thee as Incense (7004).

Incense (7004) fumigation, sweet incense, perfume, smoke, smell

The Golden Altar was the tallest piece of Furniture in the Tabernacle that we have dimensions for and its purpose was to burn incense upon, which represents our first priority that's going to bring us Closest to Jesus is prayer, even as David says.

"Let my prayer be set forth before thee as Incense". There's much more to say about the Incense but let's see the purpose of the two Golden Rings which were placed on two opposite corners first. A lot of pictures you've seen shows a ring on each corner, but that's not what Scripture says. If there were four rings, when they traveled through the wilderness and went up a hill or down a hill the Altar would have tilted and slid. It wouldn't have stayed level. But with two rings as Scripture instructs it to be built the Altar would be able to stay level as they went up or down a hill. The Incense Altar was for the purpose of burning Incense thereon which represents our Prayers being offered up to God, and our prayer life is to remain stable, level, whether we're going through hardships or trials as well as when everything is going well.

The Golden Rings are the reason the Altar can stay level and stable throughout their journey, because the rings are what support the Altar as the staves were placed through them. Even so as the Golden Altar made of wood, covered in gold, representing humanity covered by God's glory and the burning of the Incense representing the prayers of the saints, we also have two that support and carry us as we move through this wilderness. We are in this world but we are not of this world. We have been changed, we are seeking a country, which the builder and maker is God.

Romans 8:26-27, Likewise the Spirit also helpeth our infirmities; for we know not what we should pray for as we ought: but the Spirit itself maketh intercession for us with groanings which cannot be uttered. And he that searcheth the hearts knoweth what is the mind of the Spirit, because He maketh intercession for the saints according to the will of God.

Romans 8:34, Who is He that condemeth? It is Christ that died, yea rather, that is risen again, who is even at the right hand of God, who also maketh intercession for us.

The Rings that support the Golden Altar/Incense Altar represent Jesus and the Holy Ghost, which are the two that support us by interceding for us before God. They will enable us to live such a life and for our prayer life to remain stable even through the hard times. Even when we know not what to pray or are so torn by something going on in life, Jesus and the Holy Ghost know how to intercede on our behalf before God.

The Incense

Aaron was to burn Incense upon it every morning and every evening, a perpetual Incense (8548).

Perpetual (8548), to stretch, continuance, constant, daily, without interruption

The Incense, our Prayers, are to continually be offered up before God.

Prayer is a gift that we've been given from God. A way of communication that He's given us to commune with Him, not only for ourselves, but for others also. Prayer is our tallest order even as the Golden Altar is the tallest piece of Furniture. Prayer is powerful. Prayer will bring you into God's presence.

God has given us specific ingredients and amounts of different sweet spices to be used in order to make the Incense that is to be used as an offering up to Him.

Exodus 30:34-38, and the Lord said unto Moses, "Take unto the sweet spices, Stacte (5198), and Onycha (7827), Galbanum (2464), these sweet spices with pure Frankincense (3828).

Stacte (5198) – from 5197; a drop, specifically an aromatic gum

(5197) to ooze, distill gradually, to ball in drops (figuratively) to speak by inspiration, prophesy

Stacte is resin, a sap that drips spontaneously without incision, it's the purest form of myrrh. Myrrh is harvested by cutting into the bark or broken branch of a myrrh tree.

Onycha (7827) from (7826)

(7827) Peeling off by concussion of sound; a scale or shell, the aromatic mussel

(7826) To roar; a lion (from his characteristics), roar (fierce) lion

Galbanum (2464) An oderus gum (as if fatty)

Frankincense (3828) from (3836) from (3835) from its whiteness or perhaps that of its smoke

(3836) white

(3835) to be or become white

Frankincense was taken from a tree by cutting into the bark, allowing the sap to ooze out and they would return a few days later to collect the sap that had hardened.

God's design for this incense to be made was so unique and precise that it was to be made according to the art of an apothecary, a perfumer. They were to use the same amount of each of the spices, tempered together pure and holy. This composition of incense was not to be made for their own personal use, for it was pure and holy, set apart by God. The process of getting the incense took much effort, much work. Then there was the process of drying it out, weighing out the exact same amounts and crushing it into small pieces or even a powder and blending them together.

Remembering the Scriptures Psalm 141:2, when David said, "Let my prayer be set before thee as incense".

Knowing that the Incense is to represent our prayers ascending up before God, should bring our attention to the importance of this process. God gave specific ingredients and direction of each to be a like weight, meaning the same amount of each part was to be used in order to make this unique composition by God's design. Each part of this composition of Incense was retrieved with much effort. Stacte and Frankincense were harvested by taking the resin from a wounded or broken part of the tree, which would perhaps represent our brokenness or bruised parts of our lives. This was a process and the damage was done and it took days. I've heard even a week or so, in order for them to come back and collect the resin.

In our lives, damage and brokenness can take much longer but the emphasis must be placed on the process as well as the other ingredients needed to make this composition complete.

Galbanum was a spice that was extracted from a plant by the process of distillation. To boil it and cause the resin to surface to the top in order to be harvested. I'm sure we've all been there a time or two. God said this Incense was to be pure and holy. God is refining us.

Onycha was a shell of some type of the Red Sea, a mussel from inside this shell was extracted by opening the shell. This had to be a very difficult process because the Hebrew definition (7827) and (7826) says, peeling off by concussion of sound; a scale or shell, aromatic mussel

(7826) To roar; a lion (from its characteristics)

There are times in our lives or maybe in the lives of others that are so devastating that it pulls from the inner parts of our souls and causes even our fleshly bodies to feel the groanings of our spirit.

Brothers and sisters, all of these difficult times of life, whether they're ours or those of others; these times of suffering should all be harvested and brought together, tempered together, of each a like weight, and brought before God, that He would lift the load and carry you through the difficult times. There will be times when this Incense is offered and your heart is heavy and there will be times when your heart is full of gladness, joy and rejoicing. We're to praise God in the good times and the hard times.

The best example and the one that has been on my heart to share since we've begun this section about the Incense is in Luke 22:44, and being in an agony He prayed more earnestly: and His sweat was as it were great drops of blood falling down to the ground.

Psalm 22:1 My God, my God, why has thou forsaken me? Why are thou so far from helping me, and from the words of my roaring?

The holy composition of Incense was to be a perfume.

Perfume (7004) fumigation from (6999)

(6999) through the idea of fumigation in a Close Place and perhaps thus driving out the occupants; to smoke, to turn into a fragrance by fire (especially as an act of worship)

As you come into the presence of God, offering up your earnest prayers and before long the Spirit of God lifts you and your burden and your prayer time begins to flow. Your prayers come easily through such a liberty that you've been given and brought you into. It's then that the Incense you've brought has begun to ascend before God and the Spiritual realm that you're in has filled with smoke from the burning Incense and is now driving out all the occupants of distraction and hinderances that you may enter into the presence of our Holy God, which you may do with boldness, because of the blood of our Lord and Savior, Jesus Christ; a new and living way which He has consecrated for us, through the Veil, that is to say, His flesh.

The Holy Place

The Holy Place was 10 cubits tall by 10 cubits wide by 20 cubits long which equals 2,000 cubits, the approximate age of the church. The Lampstand, Table of Shewbread and the Golden Altar were placed in the Holy Place, the Sanctuary. This is where the priest ministers unto the Lord and for the people; to intercede on their behalf.

Acts 2:42, and they continued steadfastly in the Apostle's Doctrine and fellowship and in the breaking of bread and in prayer.

This Scripture is about the early church, when they gathered together for worship and to minister to others. You can also see the Sanctuary, the Holy Place. The Apostle's Doctrine is the Word of God (Lampstand), breaking of bread (The Table of Shewbread) and prayers (The Golden Altar).

The Holy Place represents the church and is to be fully functional today even as God's design for it in the Tabernacle. The priest ministered unto the Lord within the Holy Place upon a daily basis even as we see Jesus in Revelation 1:12-13; Jesus was there in the midst of the seven Candlesticks; the Lampstand, in the True Tabernacle that the Lord pitched and not man.

Hebrews 8:1-2, Now of the things which we have spoken this is the sum: We have such an High Priest, who is set on the right hand of the throne of the Majesty in the Heavens;

A minister of the Sanctuary, and of the True Tabernacle, which the Lord pitched and not man.

Hebrews 9:24, For Christ is not entered into the Holy Place made with hands, which are figures of the true, but into heaven itself, now to appear in the presence of God for us.

Jesus ministers unto God on our behalf, even when we feel we're not able, He carries us before the Father that we can be strengthened, encouraged, made new again and again.

Hebrews 7:24-25, But this man, because He continueth ever hath an unchangeable Priesthood. Wherefore He is able also to save them to the uttermost that come unto God by Him, seeing He everliveth to make intercession for them.

The Tabernacle Coverings

Exodus 26:1-14

There were four coverings. We will study the first inner covering. Its colors were the same as the Veil and we still study the colors as we study about the Veil. There were 10 Curtains of fine twined linen, blue, purple, and scarlet with cherubim of a cunning work.

*Each Curtain was 42 feet wide by 6 feet deep. There were 5 Curtains over the Holy Place and 5 Curtains over the Holy of Holies and down the backside, each being 30 feet deep by 42 feet wide. The 42-foot width of the Curtain would have left 18 inches on each side, because the Tabernacle was 45 feet. This would have placed the covering just above the Solid Blocks of silver, leaving the Sockets of silver exposed; although the next covering made of goat's hair was 45 feet wide, and would cover the Sockets of silver. Staying focused upon the main key points, we will move on. The Curtains were coupled together **one** (802) to **another** (269).*

*This is how the Curtains were joined together and made to fit as a protective covering, a work of embroidery throughout the entire Curtain along with angels being embroidered in it and looking down upon the priest and the glory of God from above. All of the Curtains were connected **one** to **another**, see the Hebrew definition of these words; they will describe the intent that God has for the church, the body of Christ.*

One (802) Woman, Wife, A Bride

Another (269) Sister, Brother, Your Spouse, One of an Intimate Relationship

This was not just a beautiful work of embroidery. God has a message of unity and even an intimate relationship with the body of Christ, the church, with one another in the love of God that's been endued upon us. That we would love one another and pray ye one for another even as His Word tells us. This is also describing the intimate relationship between God and the church, the body of Christ and how we are to abide in Him and God to abide in us. God could have stopped right there with this covering and it would have been a beautiful message within itself, but of course He didn't because He loves us this much. He wants us to know His love for us will take us farther than our love or our abilities could ever take us. Where we are not capable, God is and has provided a finished work at Calvary that will usher us into His presence because we have been made free from all that would hold us back or tell us that we're not worthy. God has already taken care of all of that, all of the lies, the accusations and the failures. God has completed the work of salvation through the cross of Calvary, it's a finished work, but then He also sealed you with the Holy Spirit of promise, which is the earnest (a portion) of our inheritance, until the redemption of the purchased possession, unto the praise of His glory. (Ephesians 1:13-14)

Saints, God not only provided us a way of salvation, but He also sealed us with His Holy Spirit of promise until He returns to take us home with Him and He has given us power to become the sons and daughters of God. God has even raised us up to sit together with Him in heavenly places in Christ, see Ephesians 2:6.

And just as a reminder in Hebrews 10:19-20 that we've already discussed, but now you can see this taking place in Scripture. See God's revelation in the Tabernacle, God's divine plan, God's intimacy towards us, His mind was made up long ago, He made a way for us.

Hebrews 10:19-20, Having therefore brethren boldness to enter into the Holiest by the blood of Jesus, by a new and living way, which he hath consecrated for us, through the Veil, that is to say His flesh.

*The joining of the 5 Curtains of the Sanctuary, the Holy Place and the 5 Curtains that were over the Holy of Holies took place directly overtop of the Veil. See Exodus 26:4-6 There were 50 loops of blue in the edge of the Curtain over the Holy Place and there were also 50 loops of blue in the edge of the Curtain which was over the Holy of Holies. These loops of blue took hold **one** of **another** as they spiraled continuously across the joining of these 2 Curtains to become one.*

Saints, we know that 50 represents Pentecost, which brought forth the Holy Ghost. Each one of these Curtains had the 50 loops of blue and were joined together to make one Tabernacle; to make us one with God. The Holy Spirt of God will cause us to be more than we are, He will enable us to live such a life.

Notice that the joining of these 2 Curtains took place directly overtop of the Veil, which represents Jesus' body, the work that took place at Calvary and God signifying the Finished Work by tearing the Veil in half from top to bottom.

The Holy Ghost that we've been given a portion of; the earnest of our inheritance, we are promised to receive in full when we are taken home to be with Him. This is what we are seeing in the joining of these 2 Curtains over the Veil. The 50 Loops over the Sanctuary to the 50 Loops over the Holy of Holies receive the promise of God's blessed assurance. Again, God could have stopped there, but that's right, He didn't. Verse 6 says He took 50 Taches of gold and joined the Curtains together by the Taches taking hold of the loops, holding them together.

Taches (7165) a knob or belaying pin (from its swelling form)

A belaying pin was used to secure a ship by tying ropes around it, to take up slack so the ship could be held secure.

The Tache of gold was to join and hold the Loops of blue together making one Tabernacle and to hold them securely together as one, to take up any slack and hold it secure.

Romans 4:17, God calls those things which be not as though they were.

Give yourself entirely to God and He's got you, God will hold you secure, His mind is already made up. He's made His Covenant Relationship, Covenant Promise with us. He will be our God and we will be His people.

Hebrews 4:20-21 Even as Abraham chose to believe God, that Sarah would give birth to a son in their old age. He staggered not at the Promise of God through unbelief, but was strong in faith, giving glory to God: and being fully persuaded that, what He had promised, He was able also to perform, and therefore it was imputed to him for righteousness.

Now it was not written for his sake alone, that it was imputed to him: but for us also, to whom it shall be imputed, if we believe on Him that raised up Jesus our Lord from the dead: who was delivered for our offenses, and was raised again for our justification.

The Veil

Exodus 26:31-33

The Veil was 15 feet by 15 feet foursquare and made of fine twined linen, blue, purple and scarlet. The Veil was a cunning work of embroidery with angels embroidered into it. It was hung upon the four Pillars of shittim wood and overlaid with gold. The wood represents humanity, Matthew, Mark, Luke and John which received and wrote the four Gospels in which the New Covenant is established upon. The four Pillars that the Veil was hung upon, sat upon four Sockets of silver, which are the same as the Sockets of silver for the Tabernacle Structure and represents the very same redemptive work of Christ Jesus, our Lord.

Brothers and sisters, the first five Pillars at the Door of the Tabernacle were overlaid with gold but they sat upon Sockets of brass, which represents judgment.

These five Pillars represent humanity trying to fulfill the Law of God; Genesis, Exodus, Leviticus, Numbers and Deuteronomy sat upon the Courtyard side of the Door, meaning they were still under the Law and if you broke the Law in one area, you broke the whole Law. It isn't until you come through the Door of Truth and Jesus is that Truth.

John 14:6, "I am the Way, the Truth, and the Life, no man comes unto the Father but by Me".

Once you step through the Door of Truth, then the very foundation of the faith you've been given through salvation, rests upon the redemptive work of Christ Jesus, that we can now see in the Sockets of silver under the boards of the Tabernacle Structure and the four Pillars that the Veil hung upon. These four Pillars that the Veil hung upon with the four Sockets of silver beneath them represent humanity being enabled to be obedient unto the Gospel, through the grace of God that was given unto man, through the blood of our Lord Jesus Christ, by a new and living way which He has consecrated for us through the Veil, that is to say His flesh.

If we'd also look straight up above us while standing at the Veil, we would also see the 50 Loops of blue, connecting the 50 Loops of blue of the Sanctuary covering to the 50 Loops of blue of the Holy of Holies covering with the Taches of gold joining them together to make one Tabernacle.

We can see God's divine plan of making us one with Him through the blood of Jesus, being made one with Him as He places his glory upon us as written in John 17:21-23, as well as being given power to become the sons and daughters of God through the Holy Spirit of God.

The fine twined white linen of the Veil represents Righteousness (Revelation 19:8), the blue represents the Holy Ghost, even as the Robe of the Ephod; being endued with power from on High (Exodus 28:31 and Luke 24:49).

The purple represents Royalty and the scarlet red of course represents the Blood of Jesus.

I want to share with you a more in-depth study upon 2 of these colors, the Blue and the Red.

Blue (8504) from 7827 & 7826)

(8504) A blue dye of an aromatic mussel, from a shellfish. Obtained by the peeling off / or force, by the concussion of sound.

Concussion: a violent shaking

(7826) characterized by the Roar of a Lion

Psalm 22:1 "My god, my God, why hast thou forsaken me? Why are thou so far from helping me, and from the words of my Roaring?"

Roaring (7581) a rumbling or moan

The blue color also represents the agony that Jesus bore upon Mount Calvary.

What I'm about to share now is hard to say and will even be harder to write, but I will write the definitions and the Scriptures that they pertain to. I want you to see the Revelation, the understanding of the original language and of the Scriptures of what Jesus has done for us.

Scarlet (8144, 8438)

(8144) a red dye, extracted from the crimson grub worm

The crimson grub worm would attach itself firmly to a tree or a wooden post in order to give birth. Once it gives birth, it will die and its young would then feed off her body, until they could fend for themselves. While eating from its body, the young would become stained with this red dye. The red dye from the grub worm will not wash off.

John 6:53,54 and 56, Jesus said, "Verily, verily, I say unto you, except ye eat the flesh of the Son of Man, and drink His blood, ye have no life in you. Whoso eateth My flesh, and drinketh My blood, hath eternal life; and I will raise him up at the last day.

He that eateth My flesh, and drinketh My blood, dwelleth in Me, and I in him".

We have truly been washed in His blood and partake of Him. We have been born again, grafted into the family of God. Our heavenly Father will see the blood as we stand before Him.

(8438) a maggot (as varacious)

Varacious – eating with greediness, ravenous

Ravenous – eating with extreme eagerness as for gratification.

Psalm 22:6, But I am a worm, and no man, a reproach of men, and despised of the people.

Jesus not only forgave us of our sins, but He is removing the sin from us. He knows exactly where it is and what it is. He will keep coming after the sinfulness of our fleshly nature for we are to be one with Him and in His image.

"Some of the soldiers that were wounded" during World War I, was found with maggots eating at their wounds, and the field medics saw that their wounds were healing better than those that didn't have them.

Once the infectious dead flesh is removed, the blood can start to flow freely and begin to heal these wounded areas.

Once the infectious sinfulness has been removed the Blood of Jesus can flow freely and begin to heal us from the inside out.

The Placement of the Veil

Exodus 26:33, and thou shalt hang up the Veil under the Taches (7165), that thou mayest bring in thither within the Veil, the Ark of the Testimony: and the Veil shall divide unto you between the Holy Place and the Most Holy Place.

The Veil was used to separate the Holy Place from the Holy of Holies because the way into the Holiest of all was not yet made manifest, while as the first Tabernacle was yet standing, Hebrews 9:8.

Jesus had not yet been born of this life or crucified, therefore man still carried the guilt of sin and shame within his conscience, because the blood of bulls and goats could not make him perfect, as pertaining to the conscience, Hebrews 9:9.

Notice, Exodus 26:33, says, and thou shalt hang up the Veil under the Taches, that thou mayest bring in thither within the Veil the Ark of the Testimony.

They were to hang the Veil under the 50 gold Taches above that are holding the 50 loops of Blue, making the Tabernacle covering as to be one complete covering, one Tabernacle. For it was God's promise to come that we would be made one with God and have full access into the very presence of God.

This promise, the fulfilling of Scripture took place when Jesus laid down His life and then took it up again in resurrection. Giving us freedom from sin, freedom from its power, and full access into the very presence of God, because the blood of Jesus is worthy to remove all sin and even clear the conscience.

God signifying, that the way into the Holiest of all, the Holy of Holies, has now been made known to us, by tearing the Veil from top to bottom, no longer separating the Holy of Holies from the Holy Place. The Holy Place represents the church age that we are living in today and the Holy of Holies represents heaven itself, the very presence of God. You and I are no longer separated from God and you are not dependent on anyone else to approach God for you. You have been given access into His very presence by the blood of Jesus. Because of this great way of salvation, of being washed in His blood, cleansed and made whole, during that quick, powerful, life changing work of God, He has quickened us together with Christ, (by grace are ye saved) and hath raised us up together, and made us sit together in heavenly places in Christ Jesus. (Ephesians 2:5-6)

If you can sit together with Christ Jesus in heavenly places, then it's a done deal, it's as Jesus said, "It is finished!"

Enjoy the splendors of heaven while here on this earth. Don't dare miss out on the privileges that Jesus has made way for you and I to enjoy now. He longs for us to be not only made like Him, but also to be with Him. He's already proved this by providing this great way of salvation and His many wonderful promises as well. Hold to His unchanging hand. Live in the Spirit and walk in the Spirit. Evaluate your living by the Fruit of the Spirit, Galatians 5:22-23.

John 17:21-23 "That they all may be one; as thou, Father, art in me, and I in Thee, that they also may be one in us: that the world may believe that thou hast sent me. 22) And the glory which thou gavest Me I have given them; that they may be one, even as we are one: 23) I in them, and thou in me, that they may be perfect in one; and that the world may know that thou hast sent me, and hast loved them, as thou hast loved me."

Receive God's promises and walk in them. Recognize who you are in Christ Jesus and who He has made you to be.

Exodus 26:33, They were to hang up the Veil under the Taches above, again meaning the 50 loops of Blue, representing the Holy Ghost. Imagine that the Holy Ghost pulling together the coverings over the Holy Place and the Holy of

Holies and joining them together to make one covering, one Tabernacle. See Exodus 26:6, the latter part of the verse says, "It shall be one Tabernacle".

The joining of the two coverings took place directly over top of the Veil, the precious work of Jesus at Calvary. Making the way for us to become one with Him, having full access into His presence, but even providing further assistance to enable us to become like Him, to live such a life as His word instructs us to.

Even as the joining of the two Curtains above by the 50 loops of Blue taking hold one of another; the Holy Ghost sent down from heaven to dwell in us. Wow, receive His promise brothers and sisters, to lead you and guide you into all Truth, into all of His ways and to strengthen you and enable you to live such a life, because you have been changed.

The blood of Jesus has washed you and you have been stained with the blood of Jesus. It doesn't just wash away. Live in His promises.

The Holy Ghost will enable you to be more than you are, He will bless you to do more than you're capable of, therefore, glorify God in His precious promises.

There's yet one more thing to bring out and see about in Exodus 26:33. They had to hang the Veil, that they may bring in thither within the Veil, the Ark of the Testimony, The Ark of the Covenant. This brings us to the study of the Ark of the Covenant. The Ark of the Covenant was made of wood. It represented humanity, us; being in the very presence of God.

The Ark of the Covenant being in the Holy of Holies and the box, itself, being made of wood representing humanity was symbolic of God's promise to come, mankind being the in the very presence of God. This was not physically or spiritually possible during the Old Testament because the way into the Holiest was not yet made manifest, but it was symbolic of what was to come. Now we have received this promise in part. We have access into His presence and yet it is also still symbolic of what is to come when Jesus takes us home to be with Him forever more. We truly are the blessed ones of God!

The Ark of the Covenant

Exodus 25:10-22

The Ark itself, the box was made of shittim wood, which we know represents humanity, you and I. It was 3 feet, 9 inches long by 27 inches wide and 27 inches tall. It was overlaid with pure Gold within and without and had a crown of Gold round about it.

The Ark was made to contain and to keep the things that God wanted stored in it. Exodus 25:16, the Testimony, which is the Ten Commandments.

Numbers 17:10, Aaron's Rod that budded and brought forth almonds.

Exodus 16:32-34, the Golden Pot of Manna, Aaron's Rod that budded and the Tablets of the Covenant were kept inside of the Ark of the Covenant.

The Ten Commandments are the Word of God and they represent the Father. Jesus, Himself, said, "The words that I speak are not my own, but that which I have received of my Father".

The Golden Pot of Manna, represents Jesus. John 6:48-51; "I am that bread of life. Your fathers did eat manna in the wilderness, and are dead. This is the bread which cometh down from heaven, that a man may eat thereof and not die. I am the Living Bread that came down from heaven: if any man eat of this bread, he shall live forever: and the Bread that I give is my flesh, which I will give for the life of the world".

The Rod of Aaron that budded and produced almonds, represents the power of the Holy Ghost and the quick work of God.

You have the Father, the Son, and the Holy Ghost inside of the Ark, which represents the Father, the Son, and the Holy Ghost inside of us; this is the Covenant of God that was to come so it's called the Ark of the Covenant. To make this possible there was the Covering, the Lid of the Ark, called the Mercy Seat.

The Mercy Seat was 3 feet 9 inches long by 27 inches wide. A perfect fit of the exact size of the Ark. The Mercy Seat sat directly on top of the Ark and sealed in what God had commanded to be placed inside.

The Ark was covered in Gold on the inside and the outside, representing God's glory to come within us and upon our lives.

The Ark was overlaid with Gold, representing what we are going to be. Romans 4:17, God calls those things that are not as though they were.

The Mercy Seat along with the two angels that sat on top of the Mercy Seat were made of one solid piece of Gold. The Mercy Seat represents Jesus.

Romans 3:25-26, Whom God hath set forth to be a Propitiation through faith in His blood, to declare His righteousness for the remission of sins that are past, through the forbearance of God; to declare, I say, at this time His righteousness: that He might be just, and the justifier of Him which believeth in Jesus.

I John 2:2, and he is the Propitiation for our sins; and not for ours only, but also for the sins of the whole world.

I John 4:10, Herein is love, not that we loved God, but that He loved us, and sent His Son to be the Propitiation for our sins.

Propitiation (2434, 2435) Mercy Seat, the lid, the covering of the Ark of the Covenant.

(2434) that which appeases anger and brings reconciliation with someone who has reason to be angry with one

Jesus is our Mercy Seat, our covering that seals the Ordained Salvation Plan of God within us, having the Father, the Son, and the Holy Ghost inside of us and the Covenant of God is made and kept through the redemptive work at Calvary, when Jesus gave His life for us, that we might have life and have it more abundantly.

The blood was placed upon and before the Mercy Seat and our Jesus is that Mercy Seat.

The angels were made of the same Piece of Gold as the Mercy Seat, to be all one piece; truly a work of craftsmanship. Exodus 25:18-20

Hebrews 2:9, But we see Jesus, who was made a little lower than the angels for the suffering of death, crowned with glory and honor; that He by the grace of God should taste death for every man.

A clear picture of the Mercy Seat. Another Scripture is John 20:12, Mary saw two angels, one at the head and the other at the feet where the body of Jesus had laid.

The Journey Through
the Wilderness

Numbers 4:5

And when the camp setteth forward, Aaron shall come, and his sons, and they shall take down the covering Veil, and cover the Ark of the Testimony with it.

The Veil was 15 feet by 15 feet foursquare and the Ark of the Covenant was 3 feet, 9 inches long and 27 inches wide and 27 inches tall to the top of the Box, the Ark. There's no dimension given for the thickness of the Mercy Seat of the height of the angels, but being God uses the cubit for measurements in the Tabernacle, my thoughts are the Mercy Seat and the angels being one solid piece of Gold would have been one cubit tall, 18 inches. If this is correct, the Ark of the Covenant would have been 3 feet, 9 inches long by 27 inches wide by 3 feet, 9 inches tall.

The Veil was to cover the Ark of the Covenant as they moved through the wilderness, but the Veil was 15 feet by 15 feet and would have drug the ground as they walked. This doesn't seem to be very respectful to something that represents the body of Jesus.

If you would fold the Veil in half you would have 7 feet, 6 inches by 15 feet. Fold the Veil again and you would have 7 feet, 6 inches by 7 feet, 6 inches foursquare. Half of 7 feet, 6 inches is 3 feet, 9 inches, a perfect fit, a perfect covering for the Ark of the Covenant as they traveled through the wilderness.

Jesus is our Covering as we move through this wilderness that we live in. He's our Shield, our Protector, Jesus covers us with His life. There's much more to study in verses 6-15 about how each piece of Furniture was covered before they moved through the wilderness. Notice verse 13, the Brazen Altar was to be covered with a Purple Cloth. The Brazen Altar was the only one to be covered with a Purple Cloth. The Brazen Altar represents Jesus and the Purple Cloth represents His royalty.

Numbers 7:3-9, There was an offering made unto the Lord of 6 wagons and 12 oxen, God told Moses to accept this offering and give them unto the Levites for the service of the Tabernacle, to carry the materials of the Tabernacle that were disassembled, through the wilderness.

Verse 9, But unto the sons of Kohath he gave none: because the service of the Sanctuary belonging unto them was that they should bear upon their shoulders.

Numbers 3:31, and their charge shall be the Ark, and the Table, and the Candlestick, and the Altars, and the Vessels of the Sanctuary wherewith they minister, and the hanging (Veil), and all the service thereof.

The sons of Kohath of the Levites were commissioned by God to carry the Furniture of the Tabernacle through the wilderness. They weren't allowed to even see this Furniture, Aaron and his sons, the priest already had it covered with the cloths according to God's instructions, and the sons of Kohath were to carry the Furniture upon their shoulders, to bear the load.

This is symbolic of us carrying the Lampstand, the Word of God, the Table of Shewbread, Communion with Jesus, the Golden Altar, prayers of the saints, the Ark of the Covenant with the Covering Veil as we stay in covenant relationship with God as we move through this wilderness that we're in, until Jesus comes and takes us home to be with Him: The Redemption of the Purchased Possession unto the Praise of His Glory.

Not forgetting the Brazen Altar, representing Jesus and the Cross that He bore for us. He who knew no sin became sin for us and instructs us to pick up our Cross daily and follow Him, as well as the Laver; the Washing of the Water by the Word.

There were two sacrifices offered day by day continually, Exodus 29:38-41.

Jesus fulfilled this daily Sacrifice as well while on the Cross. It was to be a morning and evening Sacrifice.

Mark 15:25, third hour of the day – 9:00 a.m.

Mark 15:34 Ninth hour of the day – 3:00 p.m.

I've enjoyed sharing with you what God has shared with me. I pray that everyone that reads this book will be blessed by God's Word and His Promises and will be drawn closer and closer to Him.

Acknowledgements

A special thank you to our Pastor, Steve and Angie Wymer, of New Covenant Christian Church, Winchester, VA. They have always prayed us through and have been true friends for many years. Sister Angie offered to type the book to get it ready for publishing and I know it will be covered with their prayers.

May the reader be Blessed and to God be the Glory! Shine as lights for God's light is in you.

Bobby Holmes – 202-369-0173 (cell number)

I'd love to meet with as many of you as possible. My desire is to travel from church to church sharing this teaching of the Tabernacle. Please contact me for scheduling a time.

Printed in the United States
by Baker & Taylor Publisher Services